This
book
belongs
to:

_____

Unless otherwise indicated, all Scripture quotations are taken from The ESV® Bible (The Holy Bible, English Standard Version®), copyright © 2001 by Crossway, a publishing ministry of Good News Publishers. Used by permission. All rights reserved.

Verses marked NIV are taken from the Holy Bible, New International Version®, NIV®, Copyright © 1973, 1978, 1984, 2011 by Biblica, Inc.® Used by permission. All rights reserved worldwide.

Verses marked NASB are taken from the New American Standard Bible®, © 1960, 1962, 1963, 1968, 1971, 1972, 1973, 1975, 1977, 1995 by The Lockman Foundation. Used by permission. (www.Lockman.org).

Verses marked NLT are taken from the *Holy Bible*, New Living Translation, copyright © 1996, 2004, 2007, 2013 by Tyndale House Foundation. Used by permission of Tyndale House Publishers, Inc., Carol Stream, Illinois 60188. All rights reserved.

Verses marked NKJV are taken from the New King James Version®. Copyright © 1982 by Thomas Nelson, Inc. Used by permission. All rights reserved.

Verses marked BSB are taken from The Holy Bible, Berean Study Bible, copyright © 2016 by Bible Hub. Used by Permission. All Rights Reserved Worldwide.

Hand-lettered verses are from various translations.

Photos on pages 10 (right), 22, 223 © Elizabeth Wells. Used by permission.

Photos on pages 5, 8, 11 (bottom right), 86, 90, 91, 178, 188, 189 © Joy Harmon, Wildflowers Photography. Used by permission.

Photos on pages 98, 135 © Ashley Ann Campbell. Used by permission.

Cover by Nicole Dougherty

Interior design by Janelle Coury

Published in association with William K. Jensen Literary Agency, 119 Bampton Court, Eugene, Oregon 97404.

gracelaced

Copyright © 2017 by Ruth Chou Simons (art and text)
Published by Harvest House Publishers
Eugene, Oregon 97408
www.harvesthousepublishers.com

ISBN 978-0-7369-6904-8 (hardcover)

Printed in China

20 21 22 23 24 25 / RDS-JC / 14 13 12 11 10

gracelaced

RUTH CHOU SIMONS

HARVEST HOUSE PUBLISHERS
EUGENE, OREGON

GATHER A FEW THINGS TO GET THE MOST OUT OF THIS BOOK.

BIBLE

ART SUPPLIES

JOURNAL

A FEW MOMENTS

SOME QUIET

WILLINGNESS TO BE FILLED

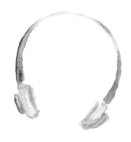

to Troy

table of contents

WELCOME

He has made everything beautiful in its time.

Ecclesiastes 3:11

Dear friend,

Cycles and seasons are part of every life journey. Take motherhood, career, fitness, education...our walk with the Lord—each of these knows ebb and flow. Solomon was right in Ecclesiastes 3: There are indeed seasons for everything, in which we struggle, persevere, thrive, and revive, again and again.

This is a book for those who wrestle with the seasons of the heart. It's for those of us who need to remember that *who we are* and *who He is* never changes, even though everything else—including our own hearts—rarely stays the same.

This book is for you...to encourage you to be deeply rooted. You hold in your hand a visual journey through some of God's faithful promises. Whether you've walked with the Lord your entire life or are just at the beginning, I want you to know that finding God's grace laced through the seasons of your heart...

WE DON'T HAVE TO BE BLOOMING TO BE GROWING

> *...begins with **resting** in who He is,*
> *...builds by **rehearsing** the truth He says about you,*
> *...blossoms as we **respond** in faith to those truths, and*
> *...is sustained by **remembering** His provision.*

This journey is not linear or formulaic, but as perennial as the seasons. Don't be discouraged to find yourself in a season of the heart repeatedly. We were made to be tethered to God's truth and not our own. Whether you are currently tilling, sowing, watering, weeding, harvesting, or waiting in your current heart season, God's inspired Word, the Bible, applies to where you are right now.

I wrote this book while sowing and growing through my own changing seasons of storms, losses, blooming, waiting, and persevering. We don't have to have the same circumstances to recognize how the grace of God is laced and woven in and through each page of your story and mine. The pages you hold here serve only to direct your gaze to Christ, the giver of all-sufficient grace for our lives. These 32 meditations are not the answer; Christ Himself is. May the words penned from my heart and the strokes of my brush serve to do as John the Baptist did in preparing the way for real hope: "Behold, the Lamb of God, who takes away the sin of the world!" (John 1:29).

My prayer is that the gospel might be adorned and God's Word be hungered after as we find ourselves in and out of these seasons of the heart, day by day, year after year.

May we discover together that we don't have to be blooming to be growing.

Because of grace,

Ruth

Winter

RESTING IN GOD'S CHARACTER

Running behind and running on empty—sometimes we find our sense of hope trampled on the hardened earth of a winter season in our lives. God calls us to lay down our frantic striving and fears to discover what might be in store for us as we wait, trust, weep, and rest.

Jesus' character—as our refuge, as trustworthy, as sufficient, as ever-present, as wise, as merciful, as in control, and as sovereign Lord—breaks through the harsh cold of the season as He steps in to carry our burdens, reminding us that true rest comes when we rest in Him.

Rock of ages Cleft FOR me LET ME hide myself IN Thee.

DWELL

He who dwells in the shelter of the Most High
will abide in the shadow of the Almighty.
I will say to the Lord, "My refuge and my fortress,
my God, in whom I trust."

<small>Psalm 91:1-2</small>

Not one corner of my home feels picked up or organized lately. With six young boys at home, we are currently blessed with more mess-makers than housekeepers, and the daily struggle is real.

REST IN GOD OUR REFUGE

Those of us who spend our days caring for our homes and our people understand the perpetualness of it all. Sure, I'm doing the next thing, learning to be more efficient, training my kids, and setting my mind on the fact that I get to serve my family. But as I press on with the things I know to do, the mundane routine of the everyday continues much like a one-year-old learning to feed himself: Some spoonfuls make it into the mouth; some just make a mess. Any notion I have of finding comfort and satisfaction in the perfection of my surroundings has simply shown itself for what it is: an idol of the heart that can neither sustain nor deliver.

A tidy home (and sometimes a calm and quiet environment) has often been my comfort—my shelter in the midst of crazy–messy seasons. It was never meant to be.

So now I find myself meditating on Psalm 91:1-2:

Turn to the unshakable, steady, and strong shelter of our Savior.

He who dwells in the shelter of the Most High
will abide in the shadow of the Almighty.
I will say to the LORD, "My refuge and my fortress,
my God, in whom I trust."

OUR TRUE HOME

The shelter the psalmist speaks of isn't made of wood or stone, yet it covers and rescues us from the prevailing winds and storms of life. When the psalmist took refuge in God the Father, he gave words to what had not yet been revealed through Jesus the Son. Hundreds of years later on a cross of wood, Christ fulfilled the covenant God made with His people—to redeem them from the crushing penalty of sin and offer Himself as the Rock and Refuge we can dwell with *and dwell in.*

Are you putting your trust and your worth in your surroundings? Do you struggle to be happy when your environment is not the way you want it to be? Have you found yourself sheltered under the wrong source of refuge? Friend, I know I have.

Brick and mortar, pillows and throws, swept floors and quiet children...our physical environment was never intended to be our true refuge. Turn instead to the unshakable, steady, and strong shelter of our Savior: "God is our refuge and strength, a very present help in trouble" (Psalm 46:1). *There* we abide; *there* we dwell; *there* we find rest.

Trust in the LORD forever, for the LORD GOD is an everlasting rock (Isaiah 26:4).

DELVE DEEPER
Exodus 33:14
Psalm 27:5
Psalm 62:7-8

RESPOND
What are the false shelters in your life?

_____ is not my shelter.
_____ is not my shelter.
_____ is not my shelter.

he who dwells
in the shelter
of the Most
High will
abide in the
shadow of the
Almighty

"MY REFUGE AND
MY FORTRESS, MY
GOD, IN WHOM
I TRUST."

PSALM 91:1-2

LEAN

*Trust in the L*ORD *with all your heart, and do not lean on your own understanding. In all your ways acknowledge him, and he will make straight your paths.*

PROVERBS 3:5-6

It always feels like it takes an eternity to get to a place you've never been.

When you're unfamiliar with the way that road winds around the stand of trees and can't see past a rocky ascent you've never traversed, you are tempted to doubt. Some of us enjoy a good surprise, but when direction and decisions are at stake, most of us want to know there's a solid plan that leads us down a straight path. We want to see Point B from where we stand at Point A.

But rarely is it so simple. Each day is filled with unending choices, big and small:

> *What to fix for supper...*
> *How to educate our children...*
> *How to have more joy...*
> *Whom to trust as a friend...*
> *What to cut from our busy schedules...*
> *How to use our time...*
> *Where to go for advice...*

REST
IN GOD'S
FAITHFULNESS

When we believe and walk in the light of God's trustworthiness, we can hardly miss finding Him to be so.

How to proceed with a health crisis...
How to forgive someone who has wounded us deeply...

There is no end to the choices we must make daily, nor a limit to how weighty those decisions can feel at times. Even small decisions sometimes have large implications—and we fear we lack the ability to choose wisely. I even recently blurted out to a friend in the midst of pressing decisions about direction and everyday choices, "I have decision fatigue!" You may know the feeling. But today's crossroads aren't meant to highlight our own wisdom or ability to stay on course, but rather to reveal where we place our confidence.

WILL YOU TRUST?

Maybe you've been leaning on your own understanding when your Father's given you the security of His presence to lean on. And perhaps your path is not what you expected or hoped for. Mine isn't either. But Proverbs tells us to wield our hearts to do what we know is true: In all our ways that feel reasonable, acknowledge that He is faithful. In all our ways that seem unreasonable, do the same.

The straightness of the path has less to do with the ease of our travel than the direction of our true destination. When we believe and walk in the light of His trustworthiness, we can hardly miss finding Him to be so.

The biggest decision you and I face today may not be what we will do next, but whom we will trust. It's not warm feelings and wishful thinking we're told to put our trust in. We're to trust in the God who led His people into the desert so they might know the end of their power and the fullness of His provision. He's doing the same with us this day.

DELVE DEEPER
Psalm 9:10
Psalm 32:10
Jeremiah 17:7

RESPOND
Where do you place your confidence when making big and small decisions?

I will trust You, Lord,...

IN WHAT SEEMS REASONABLE

IN WHAT SEEMS UNREASONABLE

Trust

WITH ALL YOUR HEART
AND DO NOT LEA

IN ALL YOUR WAYS

acknowl

AND HE WILL MAK

the Lord

N YOUR
OWN UNDERSTANDING.

tge him

TRAIGHT YOUR PATHS.

PROVERBS
3:5-6

And after you have suffered a little while the God of all grace, who has called you to his eternal glory in Christ, will himself restore, confirm, strengthen, and establish you.

1 PETER 5:10

SUFFICIENT

My grace is sufficient for you, for power is perfected in weakness.

2 CORINTHIANS 12:9 NASB

Some things aren't resolved in one weekend. Some hurts don't go away. Some prayers are not quickly answered, and some seasons don't yield the fruit we had hoped for.

But just because God does not remove the thorn doesn't mean He's not using it for our good and for His glory.

> There was given me a thorn in the flesh, a messenger of Satan to torment me—to keep me from exalting myself! Concerning this I implored the Lord three times that it might leave me. And He has said to me, "My grace is sufficient for you, for power is perfected in weakness." Most gladly, therefore, I will rather boast about my weaknesses, so that the power of Christ may dwell in me (2 Corinthians 12:7-9 NASB).

PAST THE THORN

Some of the toughest trials the Lord has allowed in my life in the last ten years as a mother, pastor's wife, school founder, and creative businesswoman have not been singularly traumatic events or experiences but rather ones that have

REST IN CHRIST'S SUFFICIENT GRACE

Just because God does not remove the thorn doesn't mean He's not using it for our good and for His glory.

slowly chipped away, overstayed their welcome, or festered into painful wounds. You know the kind I'm talking about:

> *The unresolved conflict between friends...*
> > *despite so many attempts at reconciliation.*
> *The child whose challenges persist...*
> > *with only glimmers of progress that feel like two steps*
> > > *forward and one step back.*
> *The unrelenting financial strain...*
> > *and the accumulation of bills that don't seem to reflect the*
> > > *sacrifices you've made.*
> *The gnawing pain of being misunderstood...*
> > *even though you know you can't please everyone.*

DELVE DEEPER
1 Corinthians 2:3-5
Ephesians 6:10-12
Philippians 4:12-13

If there's one thing I've learned in the past decade, it's this: We miss the lesson when we pick at the thorn...nurse it...bemoan it...*curse it.* The enemy would have us so blinded by the pain of the thorn that we can't see the beauty of the rose garden. I've been there so many times...so consumed by the discomfort that won't go away that I can't experience what fragrance of grace lies just ahead. Look past the thorn to how Christ is enough in the midst of it. His grace is sufficient for the thorn He chooses not to remove.

Friend, would we praise Him for His sustaining strength in our lives if it were not for reaching the end of our own strength?

Would we consider Him enough if we did not find ourselves lacking?

Would we know humility if not for the discomfort of obstacles and the pain of intrusions?

Would we, as did Paul, rejoice to boast in weakness if not shown the truth of our Father's seemingly backward paradigm of greatness—humility?

Today's thorn stands guard over tomorrow's rose. Don't be surprised when our heavenly Father chooses to allow the wounding of our pride this day. He does so lovingly, sovereignly, and without mistake...that we might find in Christ's sufficient grace—in our unremoved pain—the rose we long to behold, just beyond the thorn.

BUT HE SAID TO ME,
"My grace is sufficient for you, for my power is made perfect in weakness."

THEREFORE I WILL BOAST ALL THE MORE GLADLY OF MY WEAKNESSES, SO THAT THE power of Christ MAY REST UPON ME.

2 CORINTHIANS 12:9

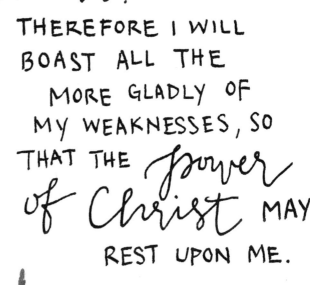

RESPOND
Write an honest prayer, giving the Lord your heartbreaks.

AND
IF NOT
HE IS
STILL
GOOD

fear
not
for i am
with you.

PRESENT

Fear not, for I am with you.

Isaiah 41:10

He cries out in the quiet of the night when he stirs awake and thinks himself alone. Our three-year-old is sixth in the lineup of man cubs at the Simons house, but he's just like the other boys were at his age: He wants the assurance of his mom's and dad's presence when he's afraid.

And what is it that I say when I tiptoe into the room to settle him down? *"Shhh. Shhh. I'm right here. Go back to sleep. I'm right here."*

My son does not need to fear because I am with him.

God spoke these very words to the Israelites, repeatedly:

> Fear not, for I am with you;
> be not dismayed, for I am your God;
> I will strengthen you, I will help you,
> I will uphold you with my righteous right hand (Isaiah 41:10).

and here,

> Have I not commanded you? Be strong and courageous. Do not be frightened, and do not be dismayed, for the LORD your God is with you wherever you go (Joshua 1:9).

REST IN GOD'S NEARNESS

The Lord is faithful to tell His children that He is near, ever-present, and carrying them through their wilderness.

33

and yet again,

> Do not fear, for *I am with you*; I will bring your offspring from the east, and gather you from the west (Isaiah 43:5 NASB, italics added).

A SURE PROMISE

DELVE DEEPER
Psalm 27:1
Psalm 56:3-4
Romans 8:38-39

God assures His people, promising, "I am with you." He doesn't promise victory on their terms, safety according to their ideas of comfort, or a timeline that always makes sense, but the Lord is faithful to tell His children that He is near, ever-present, and carrying them through their wilderness. When we are tempted to think such assurance means the way will be easy, sensible, and low risk for us, our Savior reminds us that His presence is all the help we need.

Our worst fear this day is nothing compared to the separation we'd know had Jesus not come as Immanuel: God with us. *God with us.* Jesus walked the dusty roads, ate among the lowly, fed the hungry, healed the sick. It's no coincidence that the very assurance in battle given to the Israelites by God is the one He gives in our Savior, Christ, who promises:

> And I will ask the Father, and he will give you another advocate
> to help you and be with you forever—the Spirit of truth (John
> 14:16-17 NIV).

The same God that promised to be with His people, Israel, came to live among His children and now dwells within us:

> And behold, I am with you always, to the end of the age (Matthew 28:20).

RESPOND
What fears could you release right now?

Forever. Always. The Spirit, sent by the Father, one with Christ, is with us continually.

Fear not. He is with us, friend. Our fears will forever and always find their remedy in His presence, first and foremost. We need not fear when He is near.

be
stronger
courageous

JOSHUA 1:9

THE LORD YOUR
GOD IS WITH
YOU WHEREVER
YOU GO.

pyxie

IMMANUEL

god with us

ASK

If any of you lacks wisdom, let him ask God, who gives generously to all without reproach, and it will be given him.

JAMES 1:5

Chances are, you are facing a trial you simply don't understand today. Light winds have become stormy gales, and you're unsure about your circumstances. It may be the capsizing kind: infertility, cancer, wounding from a friend, broken family relationships, or the loss of a dream. Or maybe it's not so severe but rocks your boat nonetheless, like a stubborn child who tests your patience or a long season of waiting. Despite the "various kinds" of trials that God allows in each of our lives, the Bible assures us that they are not without purpose. The apostle James tells us how to think about trials:

REST IN GOD'S WISDOM

> Count it all joy, my brothers, when you meet trials of various kinds, for you know that the testing of your faith produces steadfastness. And let steadfastness have its full effect, that you may be perfect and complete, lacking in nothing. If any of you lacks wisdom, let him ask God, who gives generously to all without reproach, and it will be given him (James 1: 2-5).

If steadfastness is the mast that stands when we persevere through trials, then asking for wisdom in the midst of them is our anchor.

> If steadfastness is the mast that stands when we persevere through trials, then asking for wisdom in the midst of them is our anchor.

A BETTER PLAN

DELVE DEEPER

Proverbs 4:6-7
Daniel 2:21
Colossians 2:2-3

How do we persevere, then, if we struggle to understand our trials? How do we move toward steadfastness? We ask for it. His wisdom is what we need, right where we are: in the middle of finding it hard to be joyful and lacking strength to endure. Asking for His wisdom is not pleading for the backstory of what we are going through, as if our Father wants to keep it from us. Instead, asking for His wisdom is aligning our vision with what He longs to reveal to us: the joy of His plans and purposes to make us mature through perseverance and complete in our faith.

As Tim Keller says, "God will only give you what you would have asked for if you knew everything he knows." We won't struggle so much with the pain of trials if we trust God to always take us toward His good in our lives. Do you want steadfastness of faith? I do. Do you want to persevere through trials in wisdom? Certainly. Ask for wisdom. He promises to give generously.

It may not be in your timing or according to your plans, but there is purpose for your current trials: to learn to ask for wisdom, to find Him faithful to answer, and to persevere in the steadfastness of your faith. You are not lost at sea in your trial, friend. You're trusting the wisdom of your Captain, who remains at the helm.

RESPOND

In what areas of your life do you need to ask God for wisdom?

His Wisdom
meets our
LACK
of
UNDERSTANDING

· JUST ASK ·

Count it all

my brothers when you meet trials of various kinds, for you know that the testing of your faith produces steadfastness. and let steadfastness have its full effect, that you may be perfect and complete, lacking nothing.

JAMES 1:2-4

joy

BROKEN

He heals the brokenhearted and binds up their wounds.

PSALM 147:3

Every broken bone or fracture requires the same thing: some kind of binding that prevents further injury and allows the body to heal and rest. I'm a mom of six boys, so it's a wonder we've yet to have one in a cast in 14 years. We've had no broken bones, but we've known plenty of broken hearts around here. We've nursed the ache of a broken heart over everything from arguments to broken toys. But we've also known broken hearts from grief over the effects of sin on broken relationships. Those are greater wounds than broken bones.

WOUND-BINDER, HEART-HEALER, STAR-NAMER

Our Father knows this. He knows, by way of putting His Son on the cross, that a broken heart aches far more than physical pain. What Jesus endured on the cross was not simply the pain of physical suffering and death, but the anguish of being forsaken by His loving Father, whose fellowship He'd only known perfectly until the moment on the cross when He cried, *"Eloi, Eloi, lema sabachthani?"* ("My God, my God, why have You forsaken me?") The burden of our sin broke the Father's heart as He placed the penalty for that sin upon the broken body of Christ. When we remember that Jesus knew grief, we

> REST IN GOD'S MERCY

> He who knows every star by name knows how to heal our wounds, great and small.

can understand the fullness of what it cost for God to do as He promised: heal the brokenhearted and bind up their wounds in a way that's eternal.

Jesus was not just forsaken by God with the curse of sin. He was betrayed, misunderstood, and mistreated by those He loved. I wish I didn't know what that feels like, but I do, as I suspect you do as well. When you and I are betrayed, misunderstood, and mistreated, our hope points back to the healing purchased for us on the cross. We get to be brokenhearted on this side of the cross. We are not left with grief that relies on earthly means of comfort, but sorrow that trusts that "he gathers the outcasts of Israel. He heals the brokenhearted and binds up their wounds. He determines the number of the stars; he gives to all of them their names" (Psalm 147:2-4).

When we cry, "Lord, do You see my distress? Do You know all the details of what is breaking my heart?" we are reminded He does. He is the Wound-binder, the Heart-healer, the Star-namer. He binds our wounds with the promise of Himself, and we can rest in knowing that He who knows every star by name knows how to heal our wounds, great and small.

DELVE DEEPER
Isaiah 53:4-5
Jeremiah 17:14
Revelation 21:4

RESPOND
List some of the ways God has healed past hurts in your life.

HE HEALS THE BROKENHEARTED
AND BINDS UP THEIR WOUNDS.
HE COUNTS THE NUMBER OF THE STARS;
HE CALLS THEM ALL BY NAME.
PSALM 147:3-4

the Lord is near to the brokenhearted and saves the crushed in spirit.

PSALM 34:18

Thou hast made us for Thyself, O Lord, and our heart is restless until it finds its rest in Thee.

AUGUSTINE OF HIPPO

REST

My soul, find rest in God; my hope comes from him.

PSALM 62:5 NIV

I've been running a bit ragged lately and thinking that maybe I resist rest because I resist not being in control.

I convince myself that my plans and dreams will fall apart if I'm not working around the clock to protect and prove them...to propel them forward. Staying ahead of the game in self-preservation has become such a normal pace in our lives that I think my heart's forgotten that it isn't what I was created for.

John Piper said, "Sleep is a daily reminder from God that we are not God." I was created to rely on Him, to trust in Him, to run out of steam, to find myself incapable of doing it all.

Unless God builds it, unless He's in it, all the laboring is in vain.

REST IN GOD'S POWER

> Unless the LORD builds the house, those who build it labor in vain. Unless the LORD watches over the city, the watchman stays awake in vain. It is in vain that you rise up early and go late to rest, eating the bread of anxious toil; for he gives to his beloved sleep (Psalm 127:1-2).

If you feel worn out, friend, it's a pretty good indication that our infinite God made you finite for a purpose.

JUST STOP

God has made us to grow weary, to call it quits in our laboring, and to rest. If you feel worn out, friend, it's a pretty good indication that our infinite God made you finite for a purpose. He is reminding you that resting isn't just a good idea; it's His example and standard for us. Our all-powerful God does not grow weary, and yet He chose to rest on the seventh day of creation.

But I'm finding that it's so much more than a day of the week or a scheduling choice. To rest is to cease striving, to be restored and refreshed. It is ultimately a physical picture of what we are called to spiritually. The cross of Christ didn't simply make it possible for us to take some time off from the burden of sin and death; it purchased for us true rest from its weight of shame continually. In Christ, we can rest from our laboring in self-preservation and self-righteousness, and put our trust in a Savior who is "before all things, and in Him all things hold together" (Colossians 1:17).

Take a deep breath and allow yourself to rest. There is no significance, hope, or value you can strive for and gain for yourself that hasn't already been made fully available to those who rest in Him.

DELVE DEEPER

Deuteronomy 33:12
Psalm 4:8
Psalm 116:7

RESPOND

Write a prayer of thanks, giving your dreams to God.

Yes, my soul, find rest in God;
my hope comes from him.

Psalm 62:5

GOOD

For God has caused me to be fruitful in the land of my affliction.

GENESIS 41:52 NKJV

You are a gardener, you know. From sunup to sundown, you work to cultivate a thriving garden. Maybe you have packets of mothering seeds, some marriage-building seeds, or even some enterprising seeds. You have big hopes and dreams, but the soil you have to work with may not be as yielding as you had imagined. Perhaps the lines in this season for you have not fallen in pleasant places, as the psalmist says for himself (Psalm 16:6), but are rather marked by trials and affliction. You look over the fence and see the array of color and beauty in your neighbor's garden while your hand is to the plow, working to break through the soil of your own.

REST IN GOD'S FAITHFULNESS

LESSONS FROM JOSEPH

Do you remember the story of Joseph in the Old Testament—how he was mistreated, falsely accused, forgotten, and made to wait? Thirteen years wrongly imprisoned and a total of 22 years before he was reconciled with his betraying brothers. Joseph knew what it felt like to not know resolution, not see justice, not see his life in bloom the way he had envisioned.

I've been finding comfort in Joseph's story lately (if you haven't read Genesis 42–50 recently, you should!), as it has brought assurance to a season of pain

You don't have to be blooming to be growing, so don't give up.

and impossible situations in my own life. As I read these chapters, it's easy to assume the climax of Joseph's story is his brothers seeking forgiveness at the end, because that's what we long for—glorious blooms. But that wasn't the lesson the Lord taught Joseph.

Instead, Joseph focused on the sovereignty of God at work in the midst of his prolonged suffering. He rested in God's purposes when he could have been bitter toward his brothers: "You intended to harm me, but God intended it all for good. He brought me to this position so I could save the lives of many people" (Genesis 50:20 NLT). Joseph fixed his eyes on the ultimate purpose of his affliction: to know the Lord's faithfulness to accomplish His will in and through a life dependent on Him.

DON'T GIVE UP

You see, the colorfully dazzling bloom is only one part of anyone's story. Blooms are not the only way to see God's faithfulness. He is actively growing you, friend, while you sow within the hard soils of affliction. You don't have to be blooming to be growing, so don't give up. *God demonstrating His glory through your dependency* is your real story, and He's writing it day by day through deepening roots and newly formed buds. Blooms will come because He's faithful to finish what He begins in us (Philippians 1:6). But even if you don't see it today, take heart. Your land of affliction is the very ground the Lord is using for your good and His glory.

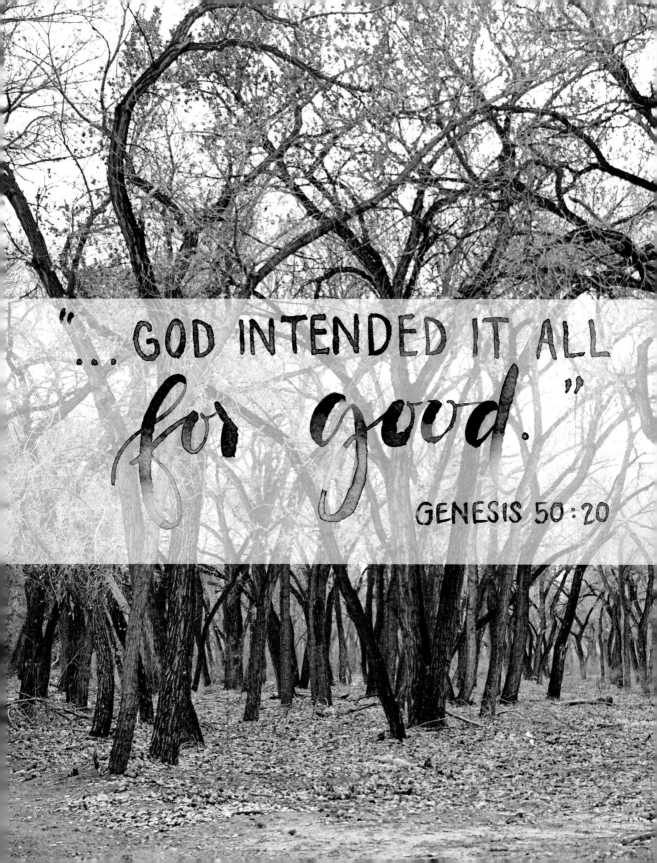

"... GOD INTENDED IT ALL *for good.*"

GENESIS 50:20

The sover
is my s
HE MAKES MY F
OF A DEER, HE EN
on the heig

ign Lord
rength;

t LIKE THE FEET
les ME TO TREAD

ts. HABAKKUK 3:19

Spring

REHEARSING THE TRUTH

Unless a grain of wheat falls into the earth and dies, it remains alone; but if it dies, it bears much fruit .

JOHN 12:24

Replacing lies with truth is where this season begins. Spring peeks out from the long, dark days like a crocus in new snowfall. Tender growth knows the wind and rain is yet to come, so it clings to new roots, anticipates the growth ahead, and grounds itself in what is right and true.

Therefore, if anyone is in Christ, he is a new Creation. The old has passed away; behold, the new has C·O·M·E

2 Corinthians 5:17

NEW

Therefore, if anyone is in Christ, he is a new creation.
The old has passed away; behold, the new has come.

2 Corinthians 5:17

More than a few times in life, I have longed for a do-over. Sometimes I've wished for it after I've made life choices that resulted in painful repercussions:

> *If only I had taken my studies more seriously...*
> *If only I hadn't chopped off all my hair because of my mood...*
> *If only I had considered wise counsel before making that*
> *   relationship decision...*
> *If only I had done my research before making that*
> *   purchase...*

And then there are times when I've simply wanted to press the rewind button on the words that spewed out of my mouth toward people I love. Do-over, please? Some things in life are easy to fix, but most of the time we can't simply rewind, restart, undo, or begin anew as if nothing had happened.

Maybe that's why it's hard for us to believe that in Christ we are a new creation. We don't always feel that way in reality, do we? We can't imagine, in the middle of our confessions of everyday mess-ups and foolish decisions, that Jesus chooses to forgive and "remembers [our] sins no more" (Isaiah 43:25 NIV), transforming us day by day into His likeness. How this happens is a mystery. It is the

**YOU ARE
A NEW
CREATION**

We are no longer the sum of our past. We are the formed and forming work of Christ's faithfulness.

work of God that, as we die to our former ways and hide ourselves in Christ, we emerge changed. He declares us a new creation from the moment we cross over from *slaves to sin* to *free in Christ*, even when the *into-His-likeness* happens over time.

DELVE DEEPER
Jeremiah
31:31-34
John 1:12-13
Romans 8:18-19

THE HOPE OF TRANSFORMATION

So be patient with yourself. And be patient with your circumstances. What you need today isn't a quick and easy do-over, despite how you feel. What you need is the hope of transformation. When you're tempted to relive the past, turn to your former ways, or see yourself as "stuck," remember anew: Just as a butterfly never returns as a chrysalis, neither do we as believers return to living as those condemned. We are not the same.

Dear friend, are you beating yourself up for mistakes rather than confessing your grateful need for transformation? Are you wallowing in the past rather than trusting Christ for your future? We don't need to strive by our own means when we've been given a spiritual makeover.

And here's the truth: We are no longer the sum of our past. We are the formed and forming work of Christ's faithfulness in us. Take flight in that freedom today, because in Christ you are a new creation.

RESPOND
In what ways has a past mistake led to your personal growth?

the old has passed away

_____

_____

_____

_____

_____

_____

_____

the new has come ...

_____

_____

_____

_____

_____

_____

_____

BELOVED

Therefore be imitators of God, as beloved children.

EPHESIANS 5:1

Two little words can change the whole way you look at your day.

No, they're not the words we all secretly hope for:

> *You're pretty.*
> *Good job.*
>
> or
>
> *Thank you.*

Sure, hearing any of those sentiments brightens any day, but those are words dependent on another person's approval or opinion of us. But when we are called "beloved children," that is an unchanging description once we've been adopted as sons and daughters through the blood of Christ (Ephesians 1:5).

CARED FOR, WELCOMED, PROTECTED

We are His beloved children, and that truth makes all the difference today if we let it sink in. We are not enemies, not disappointments, not could-have-beens, not insignificant. We aren't held at arm's length and doubtfully measured for worthiness. We are His beloved children—cared for, ransomed, welcomed, protected, defended, disciplined, and comforted by a Father who goes before us.

> YOU ARE LOVED

> We are His beloved children, and that truth makes all the difference today if we let it sink in.

73

And when our sin, shortcomings, weaknesses, and struggles keep us from feeling the reality of that description, we go back to the truth:

> By this we know that we love the children of God, when we love God and keep His commandments...His commandments are not burdensome. For everyone who has been born of God overcomes the world. And this is the victory that has overcome the world— our faith (1 John 5:2-4).

We love Him because He first loved us. Our doing what's right and true is a response to love *for Him*, not obligation *to Him*.

As Elyse Fitzpatrick says: "It is only an appreciation of his love that can motivate genuine obedience." *

Mothers know that the most genuine obedience is that which overflows from love. The more we realize how loved we are as dear children of the Father, the more we are able to respond to that love with faithfulness. Being obedient to win His favor never brings joy to the Father like doing right in imitation of His beauty and goodness does.

Preach it to yourself, beloved. You are no outcast. Live and love today knowing who you are called: *His own*. What a difference that will make when you begin there.

DELVE DEEPER
1 John 4:10
Romans 8:16-17
Ephesians 2:13

---

* Elyse Fitzpatrick, *Because He Loves Me* (Wheaton, IL: Crossway Books, 2008), 109.

lift up grateful praise to your good Father...

RESPOND
How are your
actions an
overflow of God's
love in your life?

SONS and dau

WE ARE HIS

beloved

YOU ARE NO

DELIGHT

The LORD your God is in your midst,
a mighty one who will save;
he will rejoice over you with gladness;
he will quiet you by his love;
he will exult over you with loud singing.

ZEPHANIAH 3:17

A love letter is waiting for you in your mailbox. It speaks of a conquering love that crosses every barrier to win your heart. Would you be surprised if I told you that our mighty Savior, the Lord Himself, writes you this letter and delights in you?

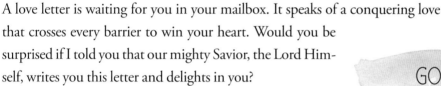

GOD REJOICES OVER YOU

I'm guessing you'd be like me and immediately protest with explanations of how you've failed too many times, how you're not that delightful when you lose your temper with your kids, or how God may have felt that way about you in times past, but not now.

I get it. I look around and see the mess in my kitchen, the mess I've made of some of my circumstances, and the secret messes in my own heart, and I simply can't imagine that God would be in my midst...and love me, even still.

GOD REJOICES OVER YOU

The Israelites in the Old Testament may have found it difficult to believe as well, but God was calling them to the truth about His love for them too. You see, Israel was just as forgetful as we are about God's love for us.

Just look again at what the prophet Zephaniah proclaims:

Jesus comes among us and blankets us with His intentional love.

81

God meets you right where you are.
God is mighty to save.
God rejoices over you.
God quiets you with His love.
God sings over you loudly!

God carries out each and every one of those promises to His people. What strikes me about this familiar verse is how deliberate God is to prove His faithfulness. He doesn't simply make Himself available for us to go to Him, but comes among us and blankets us with His intentional love. Isn't that what we see in the life of our Savior, Jesus?

DELVE DEEPER

John 16:27
Galatians 2:20
1 John 3:1

Jesus meets you right where you are.
Jesus is mighty to save.
Jesus rejoices over you.
Jesus quiets you with His love.
Jesus sings over you loudly!

We think His delight in us is wrapped up in what we do for Him. We try to make ourselves more presentable, sign up for more church activities, and clean up our act before we dare whisper a prayer. *But His delight in us is based on His character and not ours. That's the good news.*

God shows his love for us in that while we were still sinners, Christ died for us (Romans 5:8).

RESPOND

Compose a reply to God's love letter.

SURRENDER

Friend, what a difference it makes when you remember that God's love letter is for *you*. Not the you ten years from now, not the you that memorized lots of verses as a kid, not the you that checks everything off your list...but the you that surrenders to His love. That's the you He's pursuing today.

god meets you where you are

god is mighty to save

god rejoices over you

god quiets you with his love

god sings over you loudly!

the Lord your God is in
your midst.
a mighty one who
will save; he will take
great delight in you;
he will quiet you
by his love.

ZEPHANIAH 3:17

ALL GOOD THINGS
ARE WILD AND FREE.

THOREAU

FREEDOM

*For freedom Christ has set us free; stand firm therefore,
and do not submit again to a yoke of slavery.*

<small>Galatians 5:1</small>

*Freedom runs unhindered in an endless field of wildflowers.
It sounds like a mockingbird's song,
it laughs loudly, looks like a mountaintop,
feels like soaring, smells like rain, and tastes like iced tea
with a squeeze of lemon.
Freedom refreshes and breathes life into weary bones,
and I know it's what I'm made to swim in all my life.*

This is what comes to mind when I think of freedom. Whatever your own thoughts, freedom surely evokes something beautiful and unrestricted. But if freedom is so sweet and prized, why do we need to be reminded to "not submit again to a yoke of slavery"? Why would we need to guard ourselves? *Who* would run back to such a burden?

The answer is, *we would.*

I tend to measure how free I feel by way of my circumstances; I think it a luxury saved for extended holidays or retirement. Perhaps, like me, you look forward to a sense of freedom at the end of paying bills or home repairs or as a reward at the end of hard work, a job well done, or obligations completed. And so we try to manage our spiritual freedom the same way—through our

> YOU'VE BEEN SET FREE

> Your day may not resemble a carefree stroll through a field of flowers, but your burden is meant to be light in Christ.

performance and good works before God. But when it comes to the weight of sin and guilt, we are not meant to secure freedom from it through striving harder.

DELVE DEEPER
Romans 7:4
2 Corinthians
3:14-17
Galatians 3:23-29

> But now having been freed from sin and enslaved to God, you derive your benefit, resulting in sanctification, and the outcome, eternal life. For the wages of sin is death, but the free gift of God is eternal life in Christ Jesus our Lord (Romans 6:22-23 NASB).

A LIGHTER LOAD

Your day may not resemble a carefree stroll through a field of flowers, but your burden is meant to be light in Christ today because of the gift of salvation. Remember how this gift releases you to live freely. Without redemption through Christ, we are hopeless to fulfill our obligations to a holy God. Because of Christ's perfect life and sacrifice, He finishes the work that we can't. The Father forgives us when we surrender, declares us clean and accepted on account of Christ, and we are brought near. Nearness, friends, is a freedom we would not know but for the cross.

When our shortcomings today threaten to weigh us down, we return to this truth: We are set free *from* being judged according to our obedience, but are freed *to* obedience in love for a merciful Savior. Doesn't that lighten your heart, friend? You see, our freedom isn't dependent on circumstances or our own performance today. We need not return to a burdensome yoke of striving and condemnation; instead, we run...and collapse into the field of grace that welcomes us into true freedom.

RESPOND
How has Christ's love freed you?

I am free from _____.

I am free from _____.

I am free from _____.

for freedom Christ has set us free.

GALATIANS 5:1

FREE

INDEED

MASTERPIECE

For we are his workmanship, created in Christ Jesus for good works, which God prepared beforehand, that we should walk in them.

Ephesians 2:10

You, my friend, are a work of art.

Before you begin listing off all of those imperfections you dwell on, let me give you some perspective. The Greek word used for "workmanship" in Ephesians 2 is *poiema*, from which we get our English words "poem" and "poetry." Poetry is art. The best art is beautiful, unique, and treasured. The French artist Edgar Degas once said, "Art is not what you see, but what you make others see." It is an expression of what is most valuable to the one creating. Art gives form to the most significant stories the artist seeks to tell. You are God's art.

You are the work of His hands—divine poetry made to bring glory to Him!

> YOU ARE GOD'S WORKMANSHIP

THE ARTIST'S TOUCH

When God creates, He always makes a masterpiece. He is impeccable, giving the greatest attention to detail. He is not halfhearted in His workmanship or undecided in His purpose. Even the inky seas and watercolor sunsets serve their purpose, if only to declare His glory and cause praise to swell in our hearts. God is a masterful artist.

> God is not halfhearted in His workmanship or undecided in His purpose.

You have seen a painter with his palette on his finger and he has ugly little daubs of paint on the palette. What can he do with

93

DELVE DEEPER

Psalm 100:3
Isaiah 60:21
Isaiah 64:8

RESPOND

In what ways
is your life an
expression of
poetry in action?

those spots? Go in and see the picture. What splendid painting! In an even wiser way does Jesus act toward us. He takes us, poor smudges of paint, and He makes the blessed pictures of His grace out of us. It is neither the brush nor the paint He uses, but it is the skill of His own hand which does it all. *C.H. Spurgeon*

Maybe you and I struggle to see God's great workmanship in our lives because we forget our purpose. We weren't created masterfully so that we might shine brighter than others, look more beautiful in the latest fashions, or make a name for ourselves. We were lovingly created in Christ Jesus for good works designed by God, just for us.

You are beautiful. You are unique and treasured, and He's not even through with you yet! You are an expression that flows from what is most valuable to the Creator, God Himself. Created to beautifully declare the most significant story our Savior has to tell. *You* are nothing short of a *poiema* today.

Art is not what you see, but what you make others see. — EDGAR DEGAS

PRUNING

For the moment all discipline seems painful rather than pleasant, but later it yields the peaceful fruit of righteousness to those who have been trained by it.

HEBREWS 12:11

My friend Ashley prunes her rosebushes every year, and when she does, it looks like she's killing them. They are a mess, with wayward branches that she knows will stunt the growth of the roses if she doesn't trim them. So out of love for her roses, she takes out her shears and brutally clips away all that is to their detriment. And as she does, the rosebushes resist, pricking her with their thorns and scarring her arms with the tanglement of their unruliness. But she, the gardener, knows that what looks like destruction is really the beginning of beauty to come.

> YOU NEED THE GARDENER'S CARE

I'm the wild rosebush that resists pruning. Holding tenaciously to my tangle of mess and indiscipline, I flail and fuss:

> *"I can't survive this!"*
> *"I don't want to look foolish!"*
> *"This cannot be for my good!"*

And yet, I know from experience that it is loving for God not to leave me to myself.

Ease, comfort, self-sufficiency, pride, love for self, and inattentiveness to sin

> It is merciful and good of our loving Father to prune what chokes us.

will all prevent true growth if left unattended. Just like unruly branches, the very things that temporarily puff us up or make us seem greater than we are ultimately cause us to grow poorly. And so God lovingly removes those areas that keep us from bearing good fruit and being formed into His likeness. I may look like a mess in the midst of all the painful pruning and resist (how shortsighted that is!). But it is merciful and good of our loving Father to prune what chokes us, to remove what entangles us, and to cause us to be exposed and laid bare.

"When the new growth begins, the blooms are bigger than I could have imagined," Ashley tells me. "The years I skip pruning, my roses suffer."

YOU WILL SURVIVE

It may not feel like it now, but you will survive this season. You will look back and remember with discomfort how it felt to be stripped of all that felt safe but really stunted your growth. And then with joy you'll praise Him because Jesus, the Master Gardener, has prepared blooms for you that you and those around you could not have witnessed otherwise. We were created to bear fruit. Today's painful pruning paves the way for tomorrow's blooms.

DELVE DEEPER
Job 5:17
Proverbs 3:11-12
James 3:17-18

RESPOND
What areas in your life need to be pruned?

how is he
pruning you
for good?

_____

_____

_____

_____

_____

_____

_____

_____

_____

_____

and our good

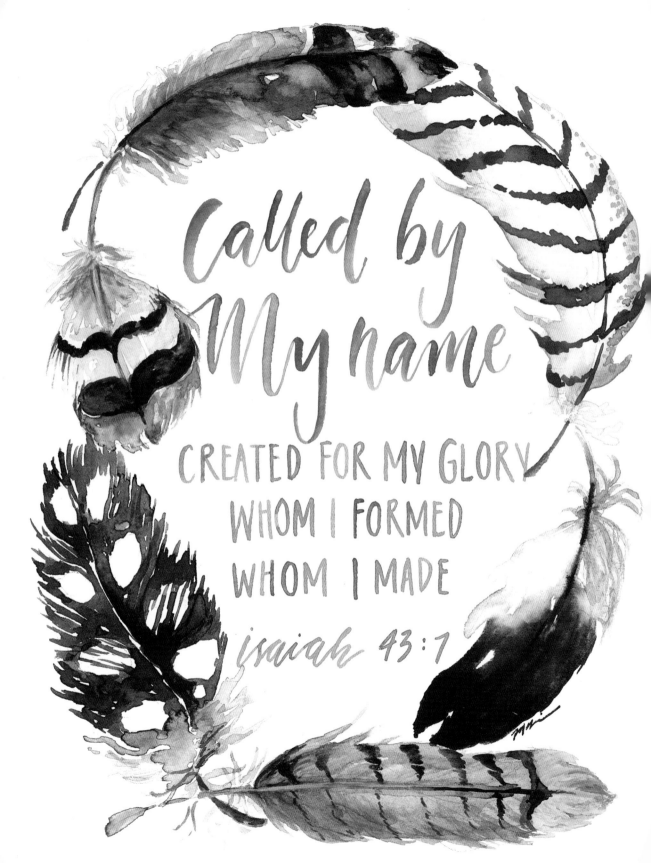

Called by My name

CREATED FOR MY GLORY
WHOM I FORMED
WHOM I MADE

isaiah 43:7

MINE

Fear not, for I have redeemed you;
I have called you by name, you are mine.

Isaiah 43:1

Nineteen years ago, when we stood before friends and family to commit our lives to one another, my husband, Troy, and I read our wedding vows and addressed one another by name. I didn't say to him, "I take you, honey, to be my wedded husband." He didn't hold my hand and say, "Girl, I promise to love and cherish you." We looked each other in the eye and called each other by name, because with that decision, he chose to be mine and I chose to be his.

I'm so grateful that the Bible speaks repeatedly of God's love for His people, the church, in the context of the sacred relationship between husband and wife. Marriage is a covenant relationship I understand both by experience and example. It's vulnerable, honest, intimate, personal, and bound by a promise. But sometimes I forget that God cares for me that personally as well. We were meant to have a relationship with Jesus, and some days I need to be reminded that I'm not just a generic face among the masses, but a chosen one whom He knows by name.

YOU ARE CHOSEN

I'm not just a generic face among the masses, but a chosen one whom God knows by name.

A PATTERN OF LOVE

Though the Israelites had not trusted and obeyed the Lord, God's word through the prophet Isaiah declared His intention to redeem His people and, ultimately, all who would come to Christ. He wooed them with His purposeful care, and we can't help but recognize the pattern of love He demonstrates with His own children:

God doesn't wait for us to be holy before He makes us whole.
God doesn't require that we be lovable before He loves us.
God doesn't ask us to make a name for ourselves before He remembers ours.

He knows your name *because* He has called you His own. He is ours because He made us His. His faithful pursuit encourages our hearts and reminds us where we stand when we don't feel worthy:

He redeemed me, called me, and made me His
even when I didn't (and don't) deserve it...
even when I don't choose Him back.

Because He redeems and keeps us, there is no need to fear. This is a covenant relationship we may not fully understand in its mystery, but we can cling to it gratefully as recipients of grace this day.

I am the good shepherd. I know my own and my own know me (John 10:14).

DELVE DEEPER
Deuteronomy 7:6
Job 19:25
Isaiah 49:1

_____

_____

_____

_____

_____

_____

_____

_____

_____

_____

_____

_____

RESPOND

How does being known and chosen change the way you commune with God?

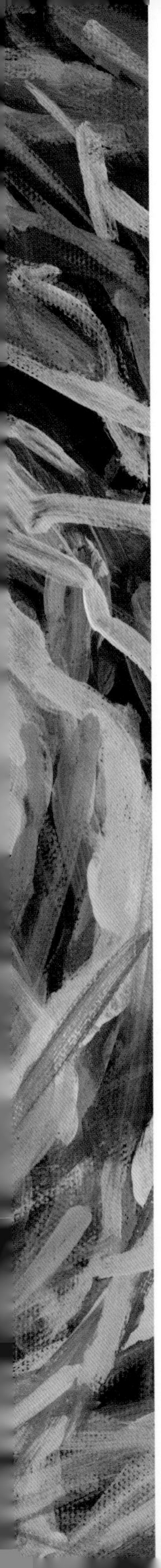

fear not,
for I have
redeemed you;
I have
called you
by name,
you are
mine.

ISAIAH 43:1

Everything
we need
for a godly life

EVERYTHING

His divine power has given us everything we need for a godly life through our knowledge of him who called us by his own glory and goodness.

2 Peter 1:3 NIV

There's nothing better than starting a recipe with all the ingredients prepped and every utensil you need at the ready. It's a *hallelujah* moment at our house when I'm not scrambling around in the kitchen for a spatula while the pot stickers are sticking to the pan or digging to find that little jar of fennel that I *know* I have tucked away in the back of the pantry. Being equipped with everything I need is empowering.

But most days I don't feel that way in my kitchen *or in my life.* I struggle to believe I have what it takes to be who God has called me to be—a wife, a mom, a daughter, a sister, a writer, a businesswoman, and a friend. I look in my toolbox and notice what's missing: patience, follow-through, kindness, organization, wisdom, self-discipline, and more. Looking at my good intentions and best efforts, I often believe I could live out my callings if I could just get past a certain threshold...a certain point of arrival.

> *That woman who's arrived looks caught up.*
> *That woman knows her Bible.*
> *That woman speaks sweetly to her children.*
> *That woman responds to hurts and trials with great faith.*

YOU HAVE
ALL THAT
YOU NEED

We have infinite resources in Christ because transformation through His Word never ceases.

111

But when that woman doesn't look like me, I feel unfit, under-equipped, and often overwhelmed. Maybe you do too?

PERSPECTIVE INSTEAD OF FORMULA

DELVE DEEPER
Psalm 23:1
2 Corinthians 9:8
2 Timothy 1:9

We long for a crash course on how to rise to our calling, but the apostle Peter gives us a perspective instead of a formula: "His [God's] divine power has given us everything we need for a godly life through our knowledge of him who called us by his own glory and goodness" (2 Peter 1:3 NIV). *Everything we need?* We are skeptical as we go down our list of missing tools, but here's the perspective:

God gives us everything we need because God gives us Himself.

We have infinite resources in Christ because transformation through His Word never ceases. The fruit of the Spirit—love, joy, peace, patience, kindness, goodness, faithfulness, gentleness, self-control—doesn't appear overnight but takes shape day by day. The truth is, we have everything we need today to live unto Him who called us to Himself if we have Christ. Colossians 2:10 tells us that we are "complete in Him" (NKJV). *In Him*...how reassuring to know where completeness is found. You may not feel like you're enough, but Christ certainly is.

If the saying is true that "God's callings are His enablings," then we are fully supplied this day.

RESPOND
Does your perspective reveal a biblical view of God's resources?

NAME YOUR
SPIRITUAL BLESSINGS:

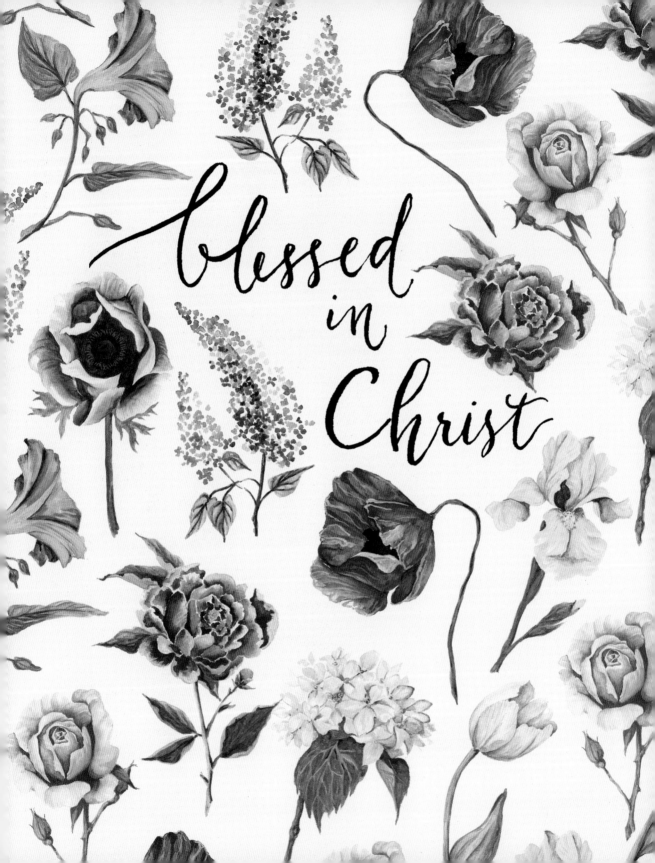

with every spiritual blessing in the heavenly places

EPHESIANS 1:3

thing

Summer

RESPONDING IN FAITH

The fruit of summer sweetly proves the roots that deepen beneath in other seasons. Just as gardens burst in response to well-nourished growth, our offerings of service and obedience can flow only from first resting in the character of God and the truth about who we are in Him. Now flourish under the warmth of the Son...and respond in faith.

COME

Let us then with confidence draw near to the throne of grace, that we may receive mercy and find grace to help in time of need.

HEBREWS 4:16

In summer, when the golden light of long afternoons floods through the west-facing window, I take a breather on the couch with a tall glass of tea and a good book. With the little boys playing at the back of the house, I call out for Haddon (our youngest, who no longer naps) to come curl up with me, perhaps coaxing a little rest on my lap. When a house is too quiet, we moms know that can be a sign that things aren't as they should be in the kid quarters. Sometimes it's too quiet because they don't want to be found, and sometimes they do but they don't know how to come without reservation. So when Haddon hears me call and comes running from the perpetual chaos and busyness of play—bouncing and eager to show me the creations he's built or the drawings he's made—I know all is well. My invitation for him to join me is a welcome break in his activities when he knows there's comfort and warmth awaiting him.

THE INVITATION

Jesus invites His own to draw near, and we believe there is joy in the presence of the Lord, our Abba Father. And yet, when we're unsure, fearful, lacking

DRAW NEAR WITH CONFIDENCE

Guilt keeps us distant while forgiveness draws us near.

confidence, or guilt-ridden, we stay away. His invitation to join Him is comfort and warmth waiting for us, but we don't always come running.

How is it that we fall at His feet when we first come to Him for salvation but then try to lean on our own worthiness to bring us back day after day? Perhaps we forget why we can—and *must*—draw near:

> *We've been given a new heart* (Ezekiel 36:26).
> *We have full assurance of faith and are sprinkled clean* (Hebrews 10:22).
> *We are not condemned* (Romans 8:1).
> *We're granted access* (Ephesians 3:12).

Guilt keeps us distant while forgiveness draws us near. The self-righteous won't come to Christ until they've formed a perfect path for themselves, but the righteous in Christ gratefully run the road paved for them by His sinless blood. They draw near with full assurance of faith because they're forgiven children, welcomed by their Father.

What is keeping you from running to your Savior today? In His presence is comfort, wisdom, strength, sustenance, forgiveness, assurance, and power to change. By faith, we draw near and have full access to all of this...all of *Him*. By faith, teach us to hear Your voice and come running, Lord.

DELVE DEEPER

Acts 22:16
2 Corinthians
3:4-5
1 John 2:28

RESPOND

Do you feel
you're running
toward God or
away from Him
today?

let us then with confidence draw near to the throne of grace, THAT WE MAY RECEIVE mercy AND find grace TO HELP IN time of need.

HEBREWS 4:16

Whatever

IS true

honorable

just pure

lovely admirable

excellent

praiseworthy—

THINK ABOUT
THESE THINGS.

philippians four eight

ABOVE

Set your minds on things above, not on earthly things.

Colossians 3:2 niv

Whether we like it or not, dwelling on the past can't change it. It won't undo the circumstances, erase the pain, solve the problems, or answer all the questions. The biggest difference made by lingering on the past is in the way it changes us, and rarely for the better.

We have but 24 hours in a day and, if we try to get our rest, only 14 hours of actively using our minds. How often I squander those precious hours worrying about the future or analyzing the past. This is the day that the Lord has made! He's made me to rejoice in it...this day.

Do you struggle to focus your mind on the present?

How our minds wander reflects what we deem most worthy—more than we might think. Even in something as essential as worship, we can sometimes forget that praising God is a battle for our minds before it is an act of our hearts. Lifting up our hands and kneeling are responses to what we believe is most worthy—and worthiness finds definition in our thoughts. We will worship what we set our minds on...what we behold. So it makes sense for the apostle Paul to remind us in various ways through his letters to the churches: Set your minds on things above.

SET YOUR MIND ON THINGS ABOVE

Praising God is a battle for our minds before it is an act of our hearts.

Why does he have to remind us to do so? Because we naturally set our minds on things of earth...

DELVE DEEPER
Proverbs 4:20-23
Romans 12:2
2 Corinthians 4:18

...our reputations

...our failures

...our possessions

...our dreams

...our goals

...our past

...our futures

...our bodies

ALIGNED WITH ETERNITY

All of those are worthwhile things to consider if they don't become what we are set on or anchored to. *Firmly planted, fully committed, deeply rooted, confidently grounded...*all these describe what it means to set our minds on something. If that something is of this world—even if it is myself—it will be shaken and cannot last forever. But if that something is of Him—of the kingdom—our minds and hearts will be aligned with what is eternal.

And so we take Paul's encouragement to heart:

> Finally, brothers, whatever is true, whatever is honorable, whatever is just, whatever is pure, whatever is lovely, whatever is commendable, if there is any excellence, if there is anything worthy of praise, think about these things (Philippians 4:8).

RESPOND
Is your mind wandering today? How can you refocus your thoughts to direct your heart?

Lord, enable us to "take every thought captive" (2 Corinthians 10:5) so that obedience, worship, and praise might overflow from eyes, minds, and hearts set on You.

WHAT IS PRAISEWORTHY?

Set your minds on thing

...ove, not on earthly things.

COLOSSIANS 3:2

Cast your anxiety on Him because He cares for you.

1 PETER 5:7

CAST

Humble yourselves, therefore, under the mighty hand of God so that at the proper time he may exalt you, casting all your anxieties on him, because he cares for you.

1 Peter 5:6-7

I see you picking up that gold-foiled plaque at the home decor superstore. Its emphatic declaration, "You're amazing!" soothes for the moment. You pick up another because, apparently, you have options:

"You can do whatever you set your mind to!"

"You're enough!"

"Trust yourself!"

But no amount of gold foiling replaces those gnawing, anxious thoughts—thoughts that you just can't keep up or aren't quite good enough.

When I trace every anxious thought back to its origin, I inevitably find my fear of failure and need for approval waiting for me. I want to be the prettiest, smartest, strongest, or best because I think securing these will give me the confidence and assurance I crave.

But they don't. I become anxious when I treasure another's approval more than God's approval of me; I become anxious when I believe I know how to handle a situation better than He does, even when I've proven myself wrong more than once. This is pride. It might be why Peter tells us to cast our anxieties on our Savior in the same breath as he instructs us to humble ourselves before Him. To lay down our big view of self, with our ability to control our own lives, is to throw ourselves on the mercy of an infinitely bigger God. We can't find Him faithful

> CAST YOUR
> ANXIETIES
> ON CHRIST

> To lay down our big view of self is to throw ourselves on the mercy of an infinitely bigger God.

to care for our worries and concerns if we don't take ourselves off the throne that rightfully belongs to Him.

Instead of "Believe in yourself!" Peter says, "Humble yourself."

Instead of "orchestrate the perfect timing," Peter tells us that God knows the "proper time."

Instead of "guard your reputation and care for yourself," Peter reminds us to find comfort in God's care and *His* opinion of us.

Instead of trusting ourselves, we are exhorted to cast all our cares on Christ. Why? Because Jesus proved His care and love for us when He died for us "while we were still sinners" (Romans 5:8). No, no...don't skip over that familiar verse. Hear it again: He rescued you when you didn't get it right.

That means...

...our perfectionism, that leads to worry

...our pride, that feeds fear and anxiety

...our unforgiveness of others and ourselves, that keeps us going around and around in worry and overthinking—

—all of it is known by our loving God who says, *Come and cast it on Me.*

VACATING THE THRONE

The cure for an anxious heart is not building confidence in your own abilities to overcome today's worries and concerns; it's submitting your heart to an almighty and loving Father who will transform your greatest weaknesses into a display of His perfect provision. When our Father replaces fear with strength and humility with honor, it begins with replacing our temporary earthbound perspective with His eternal one. It's an eternal perspective that promises true relief for our fears and anxieties, even if we don't experience it fully now on earth.

So vacate the throne and set aside the temporary fixes of self-assurance and authority. Our mighty God invites you to cast all your anxieties on Him. We lose nothing (but our pride and control) and gain everything (His care and provision) when we humble ourselves and esteem *Him* Ruler of All.

DELVE DEEPER
1 Samuel 2:7-8
Philippians 2:3
James 4:10

RESPOND
What cares and anxieties do you need to bring to God?

be anxious for nothing,
but in everything by prayer and
supplication, with thanksgiving
let your requests be
made known to God,

and the peace of God which surpasses all understanding, will guard your hearts and minds through Christ Jesus.

PHILIPPIANS 4:6-7

THEREFORE, my dear brothers AND sisters. STAND FIRM, Let nothing move you. Always give yourselves freely to the work of the Lord, BECAUSE YOU KNOW THAT YOUR LABOR in the Lord IS NOT IN VAIN.

1 CORINTHIANS 15:58

STAND

Therefore, my dear brothers and sisters, stand firm. Let nothing move you. Always give yourselves fully to the work of the Lord, because you know that your labor in the Lord is not in vain.

1 Corinthians 15:58 NIV

The fruitful season comes once a year for most farmers. They till the soil and plant straight rows. They pray for rain and give thanks for sunshine. They pull pesky weeds and fight off pests. Their work is to wait and persevere. And come summer, the blooms of their labors become ripe fruit for the picking.

NEVER GIVE UP

Unless it's a year of drought. Then, instead of a ripened harvest, the fields turn away with their unyielding fruitlessness.

FIRMLY PLANTED

Many of us know what it feels like to be a farmer in drought as we serve in the fields we've been given. We are mothers, missionaries, church planters, and counselors. We are teachers, friends, and CEOs. We are movers and shakers, dreamers and builders. But for all the purposing, planning, strategizing, and laboring, sometimes we simply don't see fruit the way we expected to.

Consistent parenting doesn't always produce obedient children, churches don't always grow the way they ought, faithful preaching of the gospel doesn't always fall on receptive hearts, serving a community doesn't yield immediate

> We stand firm because our identity is secure; we *keep standing* because the fruit is Christ's alone to produce.

change, working steadily doesn't guarantee a steady income. When the fruit doesn't match the effort, we are apt to grow weary and waver in our response to the work we're called to do.

How are we to "be steadfast, immovable, always abounding in the work of the Lord" as Paul instructs?

We find the answer in the verses just preceding:

> The sting of death is sin, and the power of sin is the law. But thanks be to God, who gives us the victory through our Lord Jesus Christ (1 Corinthians 15:56-57).

DELVE DEEPER
Exodus 14:13-14
Philippians 1:27
Hebrews 10:23

Paul bases our ability to respond with steadfastness *on* Christ's victory over sin. That means, as redeemed sons and daughters in Jesus, our everyday feet find their footing on the solid ground of our eternal standing in Christ. We stand firm because our identity is secure; we *keep* standing because the outcome and fruit are His alone to produce. So to you who are weary in a season where the bounty isn't quite what you may have anticipated: Our hope is eternal and not dependent on immediate gratification or successes. Keep standing, keep serving, keep working diligently unto the Lord. The One we serve stands victorious over sin and death and is faithful to produce fruit in His good time and in accordance with His purpose. When we know that to be true, no labor done unto the Lord is ever in vain.

RESPOND
How will you stand firm in your faith as you wait?

Whoever abides in me and I in him, he it is that bears much fruit, for apart from me you can do nothing.

JOHN 15:5

BEAR

in keeping

FRUIT

rith repentance.

MATTHEW 3:8

REJOICE

We rejoice in our sufferings, knowing that suffering produces endurance, and endurance produces character, and character produces hope.

Romans 5:3-4

I have a theory that the most joyful people in the world fight to rejoice. You've known them too, I'm sure: the family that's suffered the loss of a child, a believer experiencing persecution, a child defying the label of disability, modern heroes of our faith like Joni Eareckson Tada or Elisabeth Elliot. They rejoice in the face of insurmountable difficulties. We know it isn't as effortless as it can appear; it isn't without cost. Rejoicing is to the fighter as seedlings to an ashen mountainside. It is a choice to thrive. And, I'm learning, it's also a purposeful prerequisite.

REJOICE ALWAYS

If you ever drive through mountainous parts of the country, you inevitably come upon hillsides ravaged by fire. It's shocking to see. The sight makes my heart sink, and I mourn the loss of a beloved forest. It feels unjust and cruel, and certainly appears hopeless as I pass through. So imagine my surprise in learning that some pines actually require fire to propagate and thrive. It's called "serotiny," and because I'm an artist and not an ecologist, I'll simply confess: I read about it on the Internet. However, the process is fascinating. Many trees (pine, spruce, sequoia) produce cones that seal themselves shut with resin that melts only with the heat of fire. These cones await a forest fire. The burn produces an ashen layer on a forest floor, providing an ideal layer of nutrition for new seedlings to grow. For the forest, what appears to be devastation is often a rebirth.

Rejoicing is the seed-release party we offer back to the Lord as a faith-filled response to our sufferings.

And just as the heat from a fire causes a cone to open and release its seeds, God allows the pressure and discomfort of our trials to serve as the catalyst for new growth.

WORTH FIGHTING FOR

We may or may not know true suffering. I know I don't. But to the extent that we feel the heat on us today, let's remember this: When we rejoice in our sufferings, we have hope in spite of pain. And if we consider Romans 5, we will have hope in time *as a result of* working through pain. Rejoicing is the seed-release party we offer back to the Lord as a faith-filled response to our sufferings.

If that feels impossible, I understand. It doesn't come naturally to me in the least. I love this definition:

> Christian joy is the emotion springing from the deep-down confidence of the Christian that God is in complete and perfect control of everything, and will bring from it our good in time, and our glory in eternity. That's Christian joy. Christian joy is not an emotion on top of an emotion. It is not a feeling on top of a feeling. It is a feeling on top of a fact. It is an emotional response to what I know to be true about my God.*

Suffering won't discourage us from rejoicing if it gives us context for it. And like the forest that's eager to begin again, the seeds of rejoicing mature into a canopy of hope, which in time fills in all that feels barren in our lives. Our Savior is making all things new. You are a fighter, my friend...your joy is worth fighting for.

> Rejoice always, pray without ceasing, give thanks in all circumstances; for this is the will of God in Christ Jesus for you (1 Thessalonians 5:16-18).

DELVE DEEPER
2 Corinthians 4:7-17
Colossians 1:24-29
1 Peter 4:12-13

RESPOND
What rejoicing seeds can you offer back to God today?

---

* John MacArthur, https://www.gty.org/resources/pdf/sermons, 52-27.

Rejoice always
PRAY without
ceasing
Give Thanks
in all circumstances
FOR THIS is the
of GOD in will
Christ Jesus
for you.

1 THESSALONIANS 5:16-18

We rejoice in our sufferings, knowing that suffering produces endurance, and endurance produces character, and character produces HOPE.

Romans 5:3-4

FORGIVE

*Be kind to one another, tenderhearted, forgiving
one another, as God in Christ forgave you.*

Ephesians 4:32

My August flower beds are not what they were in early summer. Here in the
Southwest, the soft petals of my poppies and their companions eventually get
scorched in the desert heat. The best of my blooms shrivel
and curl up at their edges. Unless I water, replant, and refresh
the garden, what once were bright pops of color look drab,
consumed by the harsh climate—which apparently has no
difficulty sustaining weeds.

CULTIVATE TENDERNESS

Forgiveness can feel like my late summer poppies. The
persistent heat of hurt, conflict, or wrongs spoken or done
can simply singe the heart of forgiveness. We know forgiveness is beautiful and necessary and yet, under the sting of hurt, we quickly
toughen ourselves and withhold the fragrance of fruitful obedience. If we are
honest, forgiveness doesn't come naturally or easily, even for one who walks with
the Lord. What comes naturally is nursing our wounds, repeating the offense
over and over again in our minds, and harboring bitterness inside where others
can't easily see. We call it forgiveness when we've moved on, but I think forgiveness is when you let tenderness *move in.*

> We call it
> forgiveness when
> we've moved
> on, but I think
> forgiveness is
> when you let
> tenderness
> *move in.*

NOURISHING A SOFTENED HEART

How do we cultivate those soft blooms of forgiveness in the garden of our lives? The answer is in rooting ourselves deeply in the truth that Christ forgave us.

When the apostle Paul tells the Ephesians to cultivate kindness, tender hearts, and forgiveness toward one another, he poignantly frames the exhortation in the example and saving work of Christ in their lives. The good news of the gospel doesn't grow stale when humility bends our hearts to hear it anew: Jesus bore our sins, forgave us, removed those sins from our record, and gave us His righteousness so we could live as children, not enemies. And so we "bear with each other and forgive one another...Forgive as the Lord forgave you" (Colossians 3:13 NIV).

Simply put, as pardoned and forgiven people, we are not only capable but *compelled* to forgive one another.

Can we feel bitter and scorched when we think continually on His kindness toward us? *Not easily.*

Can we harden our hearts toward a brother or sister when we are reminded that the grace of God covers us and gives us a second chance—again and again? *Tenderheartedness is the more likely result.*

But can we forgive when our offender is slow to change? *How can we not when the Lord is slow to anger and abounding in love?*

When we remember how patient God is with us, the balm of His forgiveness toward us softens our hearts once again as we extend what is impossible apart from amazing grace.

DELVE DEEPER
Zechariah 7:9
Mark 11:25
Luke 6:37-38

RESPOND
Who in your life needs to see your tender heart?

Be kind to one another, tenderhearted, forgiving one another

as God in Christ forgave you.

EPHESIANS 4:32

Amazing grace is why we can forgive.

MEEK

Blessed are the meek, for they shall inherit the earth.

Matthew 5:5

If Jesus offered to speak to us directly about how to be happy, I think we'd all be quick to sign up. At the start of His public ministry, Jesus gathered His disciples and headed up on a hillside to speak with them and the multitudes who listened in. His subject wasn't how to do more, be more, or make better decisions. It was happiness.

I'm sure they perked up to listen. Who doesn't want to know the way to happiness?

But Jesus lays it out for them (and for us) in a way that makes no sense to our natural way of thinking: The path of blessedness—or happiness—isn't paved with success, fame, riches, or approval. It's not even marked by an admirable track record. Instead, our Savior draws the picture of kingdom blessing through a series of eight declarations known as the Beatitudes (Matthew 5:1-11). They begin with our spiritual bankruptcy and end with our rejoicing in persecution. I'd give anything to have seen the looks on the disciples' faces, as I can imagine their thoughts mirror mine: *How is this possible?*

In the middle of His countercultural statements about happiness, Jesus offers up the one that chafes me the most: *Blessed are the meek.*

Meekness is gentle, tenderhearted, patient, and submissive; it's an intentional and deliberate choice...

> BE GENTLE AND PATIENT

> The more seriously we take our sin and brokenness, the more amazing grace becomes.

DELVE DEEPER
John 13:14-16
Philippians 2:3-11
Titus 3:1-7

to not demand to be right

to be at peace with not winning an argument

to be okay to not be first at everything

to be willing to listen to criticism

to be able to hold our tongue, choose our words, choose our timing

And honestly, that just doesn't come naturally to me.

WHERE YOUR TREASURE IS

Here's the thing about meekness: It's a display of where your treasure is and who you worship.

If your treasure—the thing of highest worth—is yourself, you must guard it with all your might. You won't let anyone speak down to you, you'll demand only the best, and you'll be intolerant of others not meeting your standards or expectations. You will speak your mind whatever the cost because your treasure is you.

But if Christ and His holiness is your treasure, if you are humbled by how great He is—how amazing is His grace to save you—no one can steal your worth. The same grace that bent to redeem us makes it possible for us to bend in meekness to others.

We can afford to be meek because when we are in Christ, His unending grace is our full supply.

Jesus didn't start with meekness in His teaching on happiness; He began with our need to become poor in spirit (verse 3). He knew that for us to bend in humility with others, we must humble ourselves first to a holy God. And to humble ourselves to a holy God, we must know how poor in spirit we truly are. You see, the more seriously we take our sin and brokenness, the more amazing grace becomes. Happy are those who don't have to wait until all is made right to show meekness; they know where their hope comes from.

Are you surprised that happiness awaits those who have a high view of God and a right view of themselves? Does meekness seem costly to you? Actively consider who God is today and every day. Grace will become more amazing, meekness will become less daunting, and happiness will become what He intended it to be: *other*-worldly.

RESPOND

Do you have a right view of God and yourself?

Meekness isn't
weakness.
It's power
under
control.

Blessed are the poor in spirit,
for theirs is the kingdom of heaven:
Blessed are those who
mourn, for they shall be comforted.
Blessed are the meek, for they shall
inherit the earth.
Blessed are those who
hunger and thirst for
righteousness, for they shall
be satisfied.
Blessed are the merciful, for
they shall receive mercy.
Blessed are the pure in heart,
for they shall see God.
Blessed are the peacemakers,
for they shall be called sons of God.
Blessed are those who are persecuted
for righteousness sake, for theirs
is the kingdom of heaven.
Blessed are you when others revile you and
persecute you and utter all kinds of
evil against you falsely on my
account. Rejoice and be glad,
for your reward is great in
heaven, for so they
persecuted the prophets who
were before you. MATTHEW 5:3-12

But encourage one another daily, as long as it is called today, so that none of you may be hardened by sin's deceitfulness. HEBREWS 3:13

DAILY

But encourage one another daily, as long as it is called "Today,"
so that none of you may be hardened by sin's deceitfulness.

HEBREWS 3:13 NIV

Try as I might for consistency, sometimes my busy sched-
ule takes its toll, and my beloved houseplants get neglected.
It doesn't take but a few days of forgetting to water them for
the soil of my plants to get crusty and hardened. My neglect
isn't obvious immediately, but in time the plants' leaves tell
the story by their loss of sheen, lack of growth, and withering.

BUILD
UP ONE
ANOTHER

Of the many warnings we have of sin's effects on our lives, this one from the
Hebrews passage above is perhaps most poignant. The author warns of hardened
hearts and the need for persistent encouragement. Though I may not personally relate to the destructiveness of sin patterns like drug abuse, infidelity, addic-
tion, or abuse, I do know from experience how even what some people might
think of as more "respectable" sins harden the heart and deceive the unwary. As
Jerry Bridges warns:

> Sin is a spiritual and moral malignancy. Left unchecked, it can
> spread throughout our entire inner being and contaminate every
> area of our lives. Even worse, it often will "metastasize" from us
> into the lives of other believers around us.

Encourage one
another "as long
as it is called
'Today,'"—with
consistent,
purposeful,
unrelenting,
life-on-life
encouragement.

163

Sin's worst lie is that it promises relief and satisfaction while we grow blind to its wrecking ball of destruction. The deceitfulness of sin hardens the unguarded and untethered heart.

THE "ONE ANOTHERS" IN OUR LIVES

We are to be tethered first and foremost to Christ Himself, but God also uses brothers and sisters in Christ to keep us hemmed in. Our care for other people's spiritual health, their fight against sin, and their strengthening in the gospel is not a "suggestion." It's not for fair-weather friends. Hebrews 3:13 exhorts us to encourage one another daily. To make sure there's no confusion, the writer of Hebrews clarifies, "as long as it is called 'Today,'" implying consistent, purposeful, unrelenting, life-on-life encouragement. In other words, you can't have too much encouragement. Don't let down your guard with yourself or others with regard to sin. We need encouragement so that sin doesn't harden us.

To encourage daily is to operate within our friendships and community, making it possible to...

> *speak reminders of freedom in Christ...*
> *speak the joy of forgiveness in Him...*
> *speak encouragement for weariness...*
> *speak truth that convicts...*
> *speak warning of sin's lies and deception...*
> *speak friendship and care for the battles ahead...*

To encourage one another in this way is to bring water to thirsty soil. It is to "break up your fallow ground, and sow not among thorns" (Jeremiah 4:3). Do you welcome another person's encouragement as a purposeful safeguard? Are you encouraging the people in your life with diligence? It's our privilege as brothers and sisters to exhort and encourage, build up and bear with, remind and reprove...and it's equally our privilege to receive the same.

DELVE DEEPER

Ephesians 4:29
1 Thessalonians 5:11
Hebrews 10:24-25

RESPOND

How are you going to make encouraging others a priority in your life?

One anothers
of scripture...

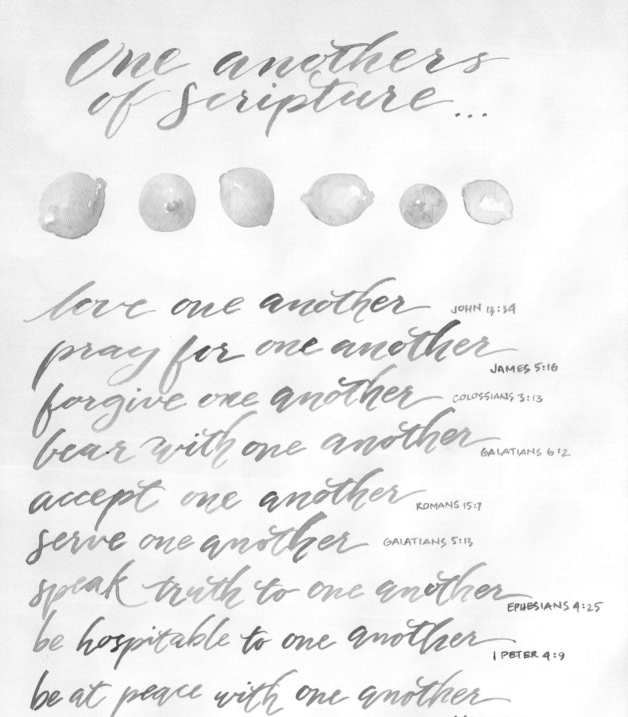

love one another — JOHN 13:34

pray for one another — JAMES 5:16

forgive one another — COLOSSIANS 3:13

bear with one another — GALATIANS 6:2

accept one another — ROMANS 15:7

serve one another — GALATIANS 5:13

speak truth to one another — EPHESIANS 4:25

be hospitable to one another — 1 PETER 4:9

be at peace with one another — MARK 9:50

Brothers and Sisters
I will encourage

Fall

REMEMBERING GOD'S PROVISIONS

Leaves turn, and the last of summer's bounty is gathered. Fall finds us grateful, hopeful, and wonderfully poured out. Just as fields slow down and quiet themselves, so we embrace Fall's changes, knowing Who supplies all things when the blooming season comes to an end. When one chapter closes and another is still not ours, the beauty we get to experience is seeing how the Father provides in the now and not yet.

HELD

Who covers the heavens with clouds, Who prepares rain for the earth, Who makes grass to grow on the mountains.

PSALM 147:8 NKJV

One of my favorite places on earth is unreachable without a four-wheel-drive, off-roading vehicle. You won't see tour buses. No tickets are sold for it, and there isn't a concession stand available for visitors. Topping out at almost 12,000 feet in elevation, Columbus Basin, in the La Plata Canyon of western Colorado, takes my breath away. I've stood at the Taj Mahal and the Great Wall of China, but man-made monuments pale in comparison to the majesty of God's declaration of sovereignty through His creation. Standing at the edge of a mountain range firmly and gently reminds me that the Creator is God, and I am not. And that in itself is where His provision begins.

Most of my unhappiness or concerns in life can be traced back to this one question: *Who holds the details of my life together? What if I can't juggle it all?*

And so the Lord paints sunsets across the skies, dabs spongy moss throughout the hills, and fills the creek with overflow that trickles into hidden waterfalls…all as if to whisper:

"I take care of the needs you don't even know to ask for. Trust *Me.*"

He's holding us together by His sovereign grace; we just need to look up long enough from our frantic agendas, news feeds, and pursuits to recognize all that declares His care.

GOD PROVIDES FOR US

The clothes on our back, equally with the cover of wildflowers that line the streams of the canyon, display His provision.

DELVE DEEPER
Job 12:10
Matthew 6:25-34
2 Corinthians
9:10-11

What can be known about God is plain to them, because God has shown it to them. For his invisible attributes, namely, his eternal power and divine nature, have been clearly perceived, ever since the creation of the world, in the things that have been made. So they are without excuse (Romans 1:19-20).

God makes us needy that we might find Him generous; He allows us to feel too weak to handle all the details that we might delight in His sovereignty. His attributes and provisions are most clearly seen through the lens of necessity, and He makes that abundantly clear to us through creation. The God who provides the rain to fall and the sun to rise provides for our daily needs. The clothes on our back, equally with the cover of wildflowers that line the streams of the canyon, display His provision of beauty and blessing. In the canyon or in the valley, "I lift up my eyes to the mountains" (Psalm 121:1 NIV) and find that my help comes from the Almighty.

You may feel as though you are juggling more than you can handle. Your current circumstances and the demands on your energy or time are beyond you. Maybe you need to say no to some wonderful things or reprioritize your time. Maybe you need to adjust your expectations or reframe your heart's desires. But maybe the only thing that must change right now is internal—a reckoning that God cares about you on the macro and micro level. He demonstrates it through His provision for you in daily details you may not recognize unless you stop to consider them: the warm meal on the table, the gas in your car, the friend who checks up on you in the middle of the week, or the refreshing rain that falls. That shelf full of Bibles you can freely open, the child safely tucked into bed, the wise doctors who walk you through your unexpected trial, and the spouse who holds your hand through it all. You're held, not because you can handle it all, but because Jesus can. If He can hold all things together—the skies and all living things—He can hold you.

RESPOND
Recall a time when God answered your need in an unexpected way.

He is before all things and in Him all things HOLD TOGETHER.

colossians 1:17

BE still AND KNOW that I AM GOD I will be exalted among the nations I will be exalted in the earth.

PSALM 46:10

INTERCESSION

Likewise the Spirit helps us in our weakness. For we do not know what to pray for as we ought, but the Spirit himself intercedes for us with groanings too deep for words.

ROMANS 8:26

To read the promises of the Bible is to know that this chapter of life on earth—weighed down with sin and ridden with pain—does not last forever. There's coming a day when sin will be no more, tears will turn to joy, and prayers won't be needed as we bask in the presence of our loving Father, our true home. We know by faith that this is true, and this is the substance of our hope.

> But for now, "we hope for what we do not see, we wait for it with patience" (Romans 8:25).

> *For now, we have broken bodies.*
> *For now, there is decay.*
> *For now, sin takes its toll.*
> *For now, we long for real healing.*
> *For now, we have sorrow in our sufferings.*

There's nothing easy about waiting, especially when we must wait with eyes of faith and the limitations of our earthly bodies. We can't yet see what the Lord

THE SPIRIT INTERCEDES FOR US

The Holy Spirit lifts us up before the Father with prayers we don't even know how to pray.

sees or know what the Lord knows. We want to pray, but sometimes life can be so complex that we even struggle to have the right words to bring to Him.

Jesus taught His disciples to pray for faith, wisdom, forgiveness, daily bread, and for strength to withstand temptation. We know to pray as Jesus taught and for His will to be done. But the apostle Paul recognized that while in the midst of our earthly struggles, suffering, ruin of sin, and not-yet-redeemed bodies, we come up short in even knowing how to ask, "Your kingdom come, Your will be done."

That's when the Holy Spirit—the third Person of the Trinity, our Counselor, and the indwelling of Christ—lifts us up before the Father with prayers we don't even know how to pray in our own wisdom. He provides the intercession that we are unable to produce. We groan as we try to pray through life's hardest challenges, while the Spirit groans on our behalf with perfect expression of our every need in the presence of our heavenly Father. The Spirit bolsters the homeward (heavenward) heart so that we might be found as John Bunyan describes:

> In prayer it is better to have a heart without words than words without a heart.

The Spirit holds us securely as we walk through the rubble of earth toward the glory of His presence, no matter how weak we feel along the long and bumpy road. Because He takes us before the throne of God day by day, moment by moment, we know we don't walk alone. The Spirit is indeed our Helper (John 14:26), both in our hearts and in connecting ours to His own. He makes prayer not just possible but plentiful as He provides for all the longings we express, and those we cannot.

DELVE DEEPER
Deuteronomy 2:7
John 14:26
Romans 15:13

RESPOND
In what areas might the Holy Spirit be interceding for you?

Our
Father
in heaven, hallowed be your name. Your kingdom come. Your will be done, on earth as it is in heaven. Give us this day our daily bread, and forgive us our debts, as we also have forgiven our debtors. And lead us not into temptation, but deliver us from evil. For yours is the kingdom, the power and the glory forevermore. Amen.

MATTHEW 6:9-13

prayer is not overcoming God's reluctance, but laying hold of His willingness.

MARTIN LUTHER

CARRIED

You will find rest for your souls. For my yoke is easy, and my burden is light.

Matthew 11:29-30

"What can I take off your plate?" he says to me as I sob.

My husband, Troy, has said these words to me on more than a few occasions when life has felt overwhelming to me as a wife and mom. Just the suggestion is often enough to soothe. I married a good one—he always follows up by taking over kitchen duties or bedtime routines and giving me a shoulder to cry on.

"Let me lighten your load. I'm happy to carry that for you—that's what these arms are for," he's been known to say with a smile...for bags of groceries and heavy hearts alike.

But the strongest arms can't carry the load Jesus refers to in Matthew 11. Jesus was speaking to the people of Israel, who were burdened by the weight of legalism and performance imposed on them by the Pharisees. The legalistic dos and don'ts of the religious leaders were crushing them. Jesus came to proclaim a path to freedom that could never be acquired by physical, mental, or religious prowess, but only by confessing one's inability to be righteous enough for a holy God: "None is righteous, no, not one" (Romans 3:10).

The burden of sin and its consequences cannot be matched by your smarts, your strength, or even your resolve for righteous living. We are experts at making light of our burdens through distractions of stuff, schedules, and social pursuits,

JESUS CARRIES OUR BURDENS

"Let me lighten your load. I'm happy to carry that for you— that's what these arms are for."

but then we wonder why we find those diversions incapable of providing comfort for our souls. I know because I've tried and come up short, time and time again.

SHOULDERING THE LOAD

You and I think that the burdens we carry today are about the circumstances in our lives—our finances, our friendships, our families, our fears. That's not untrue, but friend, would our earthly burdens feel so heavy if we stopped to acknowledge His provision for our eternal needs? Our everyday burdens are reminders that we were not designed to shoulder any of our burdens in our own strength; in fact, we were meant to let Jesus carry them on our behalf.

And Jesus comes to us today—as He did on the cross 2000 years ago—offering an unburdened soul to us who lay our baggage at His feet and take up the yoke of rest He provides. Will you lay it down? Will you take His easy yoke? With nail-scarred hands, He provides His strength in exchange for our weariness and reminds us to let Him carry us. That's what His outstretched arms are for.

DELVE DEEPER
Psalm 55:22
Psalm 68:19
Galatians 6:2

RESPOND
Create a list of
the ways God
provides for you.

it
is
finished.

When God places a burden upon you, He places His arms underneath you.

CHARLES HADDON SPURGEON

light for
my path

LIGHT

Your word is a lamp to my feet and a light to my path.

PSALM 119:105

Walking through the woods in the daytime is a completely different experience than finding our way in the night. We fear what we don't know and can't see, don't we? Light and sight play into our sense of assurance. Everything changes when the road ahead is unclear—in the groves of life as well as in the darkened woods.

> *"Show us which way to go, Lord,"* we say.
> *"What should we do?"* we ask.

If only we knew for sure whether to go left or right, to say yes or no, to stop or keep fighting, to respond or be silent, to stay or go...to step up or step down.

GOD LIGHTS OUR PATH

JUST ENOUGH LIGHT

Just tell me how to avoid all pain and experience all the best, my heart cries if I'm honest.

But as it turns out, we might ask for an unmistakably clear path only to receive light for just the next step. God's Word opens our eyes step-by-step, giving us enough light to stay on track, but not so much that we run ahead of where He's leading. You see, your Father is after your dependency, not your perfect discernment. He is more interested in your desperate need for His lamp-lit direction than in your path-paving skills. He's after your heart and offers His

God is more interested in your desperate need for His lamp-lit direction than in your path-paving skills.

Word as an invitation—not just to clear directions, but to the delight of walking with Him:

> The law of the LORD is perfect,
>   reviving the soul;
> the testimony of the LORD is sure,
>   making wise the simple;
> the precepts of the LORD are right,
>   rejoicing the heart;
> the commandment of the LORD is pure,
>   enlightening the eyes;
> the fear of the LORD is clean,
>   enduring forever;
> the rules of the LORD are true,
>   and righteous altogether.
> More to be desired are they than gold,
>   even much fine gold;
> sweeter also than honey
>   and drippings of the honeycomb (Psalm 19:7-10).

These words of David flow from a man who found God's Word to be the way to God's heart and to the reviving of his own.

Friend, it is not the dark that is our foe but rather our self-reliance. The Lord doesn't promise the removal of the darkness but the assurance of His guidance in the midst of it. His Word gives us eyes to see our circumstances

> as they really are—*under His care,*
> to consider the path as it truly is—*under His control,*
> and to see Him for who He is—*the same faithful Savior in the light of day as during the darkest night.*

Turn to the Word when you're squinting to see. He gives sight to our feeble eyes and light for our paths.

DELVE DEEPER
Psalm 32:8
Psalm 37:23
John 1:5

RESPOND
In what area do you need God more than you need answers today?

The law of the Lord is perfect,
reviving to the soul;
the testimony of the Lord is sure,
making wise the simple;
the precepts of the Lord are right,
rejoicing the heart
the commandment of the Lord is pure,
enlighting the eyes;
the fear of the Lord is clean,
enduring forever;
the rules of the Lord are true,
and righteous altogether.
More to be desired are they than gold,
even much fine gold;
sweeter also than honey
and drippings of the honeycomb.

PSALM 19 : 7-10

Your word is a lamp to my feet

and a light for my path.

PSALM 119:105

PEACE

You keep him in perfect peace whose mind is stayed on you, because he trusts in you.

Isaiah 26:3

Twelve miles out from the town of Durango, Colorado, sits a quiet piece of property where the majority of this book has been written and painted. Under the endless sky and on the acres wild, you won't find the buzz of traffic or street-lights. It's truly a bit of peace and quiet. It's restful, but the truth is, peace may be obtained by a change of location, but it can't be sustained that way. Not even the loveliest vistas can sustain the peace we need...

> *as we train up young ones who fight all day...*
> *as we navigate breaking news on social media...*
> *as we hear of injustice we feel so helpless to defend...*
> *as we face decisions for our future...*
> *as we wait for test results...*
> *as we wrestle our own shortcomings...*

JESUS IS OUR PEACE

Busy, buzzing, and anxious thoughts follow us because peace is not based on the circumstances we think about but the truth we steady our minds upon. If we fix our minds on all that might go wrong, we will anxiously work to never miss a step. We will trust in ourselves, calculate every move, and worry about what we can't know. But when we fix our minds on Jesus and trust Him, we find He gives

We can experience no true peace when we're at war with God.

197

lasting peace that He not only secures but sustains. Jesus told us that it would be unlike anything else disguised as peace from any other source:

> Peace I leave with you; my peace I give to you. Not as the world gives do I give to you. Let not your hearts be troubled, neither let them be afraid (John 14:27).

The peace Jesus offers begins with being reconciled to God through faith and forgiveness in Christ. We can experience no true peace when we're at war with God. But the peace our Father provides isn't just a cease-fire; it is a sustaining peace "like a river" (Isaiah 66:12) that promises to overflow with help and hope. He keeps us in perfect peace because His peace-giving is active and intimate as we abide in Him, and He with us...as our minds *stay* on Him.

What assurance we can have in knowing that we're not responsible to keep ourselves at peace through just the right combination of skill and strategy. It's only for us to fix our minds on His trustworthiness and then act on that perspective by *trusting Him*. Don't look simply to how He provides in your circumstances, friend—consider how He provides *for you* to walk through them. He does the keeping...He keeps the peace.

DELVE DEEPER
Isaiah 9:6
Matthew 10:29-30
Philippians 4:7

RESPOND
What holds you back from experiencing God's peace?

_____ holds me back

_____ holds me back

_____ holds me back

THE LORD BLESS YOU
AND KEEP YOU;
THE LORD MAKE
HIS FACE SHINE
ON YOU;
AND BE GRACIOUS
TO YOU;
THE LORD TURN
HIS FACE TOWARD YOU
AND GIVE YOU
PEACE.

NUMBERS 6:24-26

When peace like a river
    attendeth my way
When sorrows like sea
    billows roll;
Whatever my lot, Thou has
    taught me to say,
It is well, it is well with
    my soul.
My sin — oh, the bliss of this
    glorious thought! —
My sin, not in part but
    the whole, is nailed to
    the cross, and I bear it no more,
Praise the Lord, Praise the
    Lord, O my soul!

HORATIO G. SPAFFORD

Even though I walk
through the valley of
the shadow of death,
I will fear no evil,
for you are with me;
your rod and your staff
they comfort me.

Surely goodness and mercy
shall follow me all the days
of my life, and I shall
dwell in the house of the
Lord forever. PSALM 23

LED

He leads me beside quiet waters, he refreshes my soul.
He guides me along the right paths for his name's sake.
Even though I walk through the darkest valley.

PSALM 23:2-4 NIV

Given a choice, most of us will take the path of least resistance. No one volunteers for a life of reoccurring obstacles, a road of suffering, a trudge through tragedy, or a drive along the edge of unknowns. "Take us anywhere but *there,* Lord," we pray. We are grateful for the Lord's leading when He guides us into security, prosperity, blessing, and health, but we are resistant to follow when His leading takes us where sunshine is scarce—through the valley.

GOD LEADS US

We may not want to picture ourselves as vulnerable and in need of leading, but that's exactly how Psalm 23 describes our walk with the Lord. Of all the beloved psalms, Psalm 23 brings special comfort as we journey through the seasons of life. We're reminded that we are sheep who need a Shepherd; we are lost without Him. Our Good Shepherd leads us to nourishing pastures. He guides us in wisdom and prepares our paths. But the same protecting Shepherd, our Lord Jesus, also takes us through valleys deep.

We are sheep who need a Shepherd; we are lost without Him.

Do we question His faithfulness when we can't see the other side of a mountain's stern face? Do we wonder if His staff and rod can truly comfort when the warmth of the sun isn't on our backs? The psalmist tells us that our faithful Lord

203

who refreshes our souls is the same One who walks with us through dark times—times we're tempted to fear.

THE DARK VALLEY

The dark valley is where we struggle to gain ground and perspective. For sheep without a shepherd, the valley is an unprotected place of unknowns and unsure footing. What is a sheep to do when she has no guardian or leader? She must look to her own resources for protection and survival. She attempts to guard herself and outsmart her enemy. She acts brave though she fears.

But for us who know our Shepherd's voice and His guiding staff, our trust is in Him and not in ourselves. Every stream for our thirst, every pasture for our rest, and every safe passage through the valley is a testament to His leading. For the sheep belonging to the Shepherd, even the canyon is His provision because we learn to follow His lead like sheep when we don't know the way. We don't anxiously protect ourselves because He is our Protector. We go with confidence because He goes before us and prepares a table of blessings. We have no enemy to fear because our Shepherd is near.

We may not sign up for the darkest valley, but we can know the mercy and goodness of the One who leads us in and through it. And that safe passage, in the shape of the Good Shepherd, is ours each day as we follow Him…all the days of our lives.

DELVE DEEPER

Deuteronomy
31:8
Proverbs 16:9
Isaiah 58:11

RESPOND

What situation
are you in that
needs the
Shepherd's care?

Savior like a shepherd
lead us, much we
need Thy tender
care;
In Thy pleasant
pastures feed us,
for our use Thy
folds prepare
Blessed Jesus,
blessed Jesus;
Thou hast bought
us, Thine we are.

the
path of life

PURPOSE

You make known to me the path of life.

Psalm 16:11

Have you ever tried to persevere in a difficult task without a clear purpose or objective? It's unnerving, and discouragement always lurks about when we don't know where we're heading or why. Without purpose, our effort toward any finish line rests on our moment-by-moment feelings.

Life doesn't always *feel* purposeful, and the clarity for that purpose isn't always at our fingertips day to day.

Who made me? Why am I here? What is my purpose? These are questions that each of us asks when everyday rhythms feel monotonous and insignificant— or when life's crossroads seem *too* significant, and we stretch to understand how we fit.

Our culture tells us that our purpose is to acquire all the best this life can offer and to seek our own pleasure like the rich fool in the parable in Luke 12: "Then I will say to myself, 'You have plenty of good things laid up for many years. Take it easy. Eat, drink, and be merry!'" (verse 19 BSB). But Jesus called this thinking foolish. We are reminded instead that God "created all things, and by [His] will they existed and were created" (Revelation 4:11) and that He declared to His people:

> But for this purpose I have raised you up, to show you my power,
> so that my name may be proclaimed in all the earth (Exodus 9:16).

GOD GIVES US PURPOSE

You were created *on purpose* and *for purpose.*

209

CREATED FOR GOD'S GLORY

Simply put, you were created *on purpose* and *for purpose*. God, Who made you to be, is not passive about why you're here. He takes pleasure in His creation (you!) and created you for His glory (Isaiah 43:7). It's by Him, for Him, and to His glory that you exist (Romans 11:36).

Instead of finding our purpose in hoarding the best of this life on earth for our own pleasure within it, we've been freely given the best of eternal life through communion with Christ and His great pleasure in us.

Our Father made us, saved us, and sanctifies us daily to glorify Him...

> *as image bearers* (Genesis 1:27)
>
> *as imitators of Christ* (Ephesians 5:1-2)
>
> *as ambassadors* (2 Corinthians 5:20)
>
> *as salt and light* (Matthew 5:13-16)
>
> *as doers of good works* (Ephesians 2:10)
>
> *as disciple makers* (Matthew 28:19)

DELVE DEEPER

Psalm 138:8
Romans 8:28
1 Peter 2:9

None of these positions of purpose can exist apart from God's provision to fulfill them. You and I have purpose today because He declares it. In the most mundane and the most magical seasons alike, our purpose does not change.

"What is the chief end of man?" asks the first question of the Westminster Shorter Catechism. And succinctly, it answers: *"The chief purpose for which man is made is to glorify God, and to enjoy him forever."*

To glorify Him by loving Him...to glorify Him *because we love Him.*

RESPOND

How can you align your purpose with God's purpose for you?

> You make known to me the path of life;
>
> in your presence there is fullness of joy;
>
> at your right hand are pleasures forevermore (Psalm 16:11).

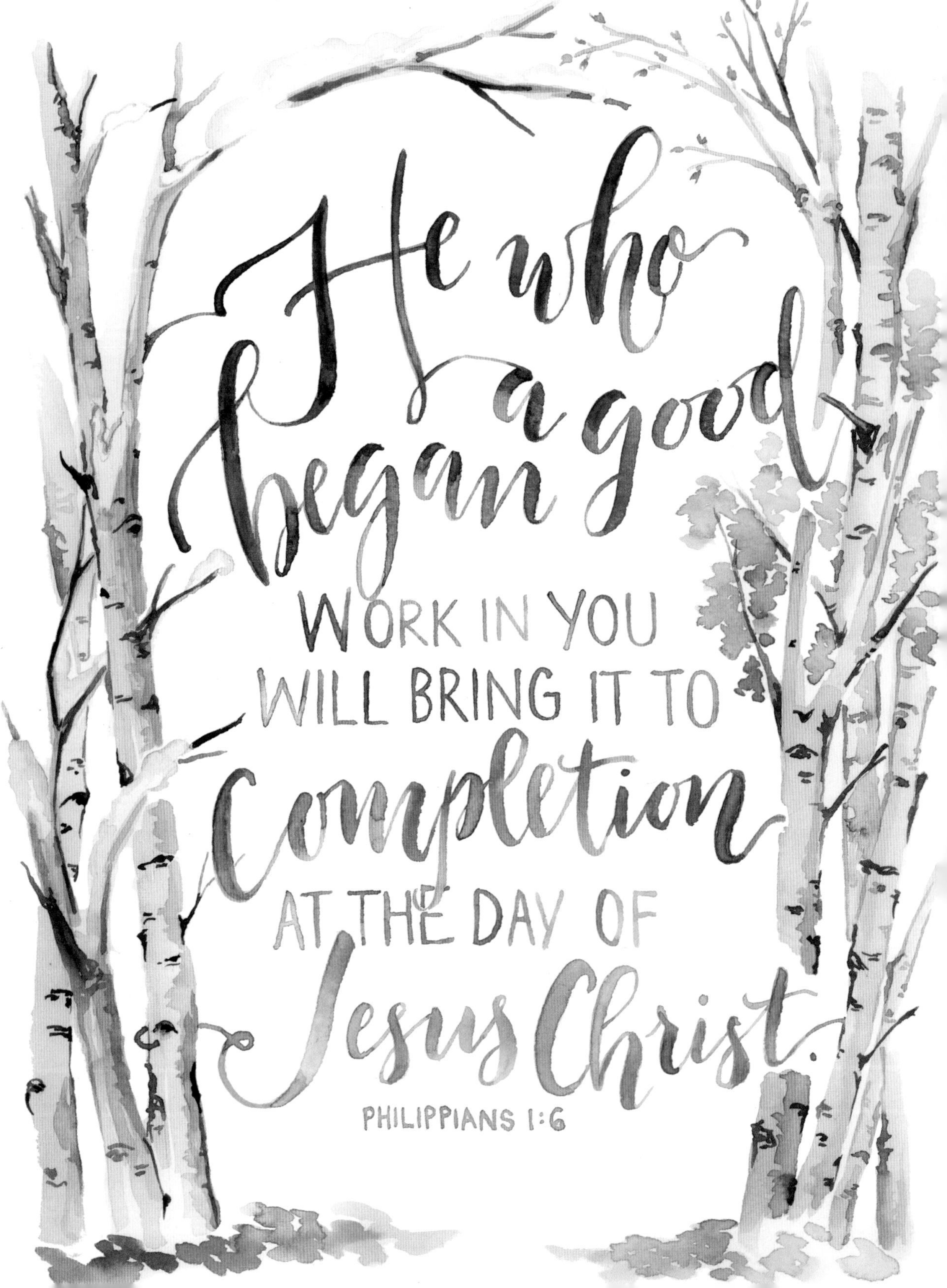

He who
began a good
WORK IN YOU
WILL BRING IT TO
completion
AT THE DAY OF
Jesus Christ.
PHILIPPIANS 1:6

ASSURANCE

He who began a good work in you will bring it to completion at the day of Jesus Christ.

Philippians 1:6

Sometimes this life of discipleship, of walking the narrow road, feels like returning from a road trip: mile after mile...*so close, but not yet home.*

We recognize the street signs, and there's even comfort in knowing that where we are is not where we'll be. We know where we're heading, but still the waiting is hard as we journey home. The road heavenward as a child of God feels this way to me most days. I know what awaits me, but I long for it to be real, now.

GOD GIVES US ASSURANCE

> *I want zero reasons to cry.*
> *I want a redeemed body.*
> *I want to sin no more.*
> *I want total healing.*
> *I want the end of darkness.*
> *I want fullness of joy.*
> *I want self-forgetfulness.*
> *I want the end of lies, hate, and pain.*
> *I want pure worship.*

Our Savior is our surety—our guarantor—of the gift of grace. He has perfect follow-through. He doesn't fail.

215

I want real unity between people of all colors, tribes, and nations.
I want to see Jesus face-to-face.

I want all that God promises in the new heaven and the new earth. We know what awaits us, but sometimes the terrain is unsure and the fog rolls in, so we strain to see and even wonder if we will ever complete the journey home.

Perhaps that's why the apostle Paul encouraged the Philippians with the assurance that Christ would follow through in the lives of believers. Paul knew that we, like the church in Philippi, could be weary and impatient travelers if we didn't see results or sense relief. Paul wrote his letter while facing death in imprisonment. He knew something of trusting the faithfulness of his Lord, Jesus, amidst unresolved realities and unsure outcomes.

Paul's words assure us that Christ is both the Author of the new life in us through redemption and the One who brings it to completion...perfected, finished, whole, and lacking nothing. Day by day, moment by moment, mile by mile, the Lord wastes nothing of our waiting and longing for home: "He will also keep you firm to the end, so that you will be blameless on the day of our Lord Jesus Christ" (1 Corinthians 1:8 NIV).

Friend, do not rely on merely what your eyes can or cannot see, or what your bones so confidently feel. Look for fruit, test your faith, and study to show yourself approved (2 Timothy 2:15), yes, but rejoice that His work to sanctify you is steady and true, even when you're tired of waiting.

Our Savior is our surety—our guarantor—of the gift of grace (Hebrews 7:22) that made us His. He has perfect follow-through. He doesn't fail. Because His Word is guaranteed by His shed blood, and His blood is guaranteed by the holiness and goodness of the God who will wipe away every tear and welcome us into His presence on the day of His coming, we have assurance that we will not only make it home, we will arrive ready and complete.

DELVE DEEPER
Deuteronomy 31:6
Galatians 6:9
James 1:12

RESPOND
Write a prayer of thanks as you rest in faith.

HE WILL WIPE EVERY TEAR FROM THEIR EYES, AND DEATH SHALL BE NO MORE, NEITHER SHALL THERE BE MOURNING, NOR CRYING, NOR PAIN ANYMORE, FOR THE FORMER THINGS HAVE PASSED AWAY.

"behold, I am making all things new."

REVELATION 21:4-5

Come to Me,
all who are
weary and
heavy-laden,
and I will
give you rest.

MATTHEW 11:28

an invitation

For those who are beginning at the end...

Welcome.

You may be reading these words of God's faithfulness in salvation and transformation and find yourself on the outside looking in. Or perhaps the religious road you've been on doesn't feel much like the grace of God you are reading about here or in God's Word. Maybe you've tasted and seen the grace of God and today is your new beginning to walk in that grace, each and every season of the heart.

The gospel—the good news of Jesus Christ—is simply this:

the end to earning His favor	*a beginning in surrender*
the end to self-reliance	*a beginning in forgiveness*
the end to slavery to sin	*a beginning in holiness*
the end to condemnation	*a beginning in freedom*
the end to being good enough	*a beginning in loving Christ more*

A love story told from the beginning of time begins in the garden, where Adam and Eve knew no separation from their Creator until they exchanged transparency with their God for sinful pride. It's the story of how that same God orchestrated and wooed His people for generations that they might know the weight of their sin and their need for a Savior. That Savior was Jesus, who lived a sinless life for 33 years on earth in order to fulfill the will of the Father by dying a criminal's death on the cross to pay the penalty of man's disobedience—the penalty of separation that you and I would suffer if not for the shed blood of Christ. And so the invitation and welcome is yours: to come as broken, hopeless, and burdened...and find peace for your soul.

Here's to your new beginning,

Ruth

About Ruth and the gracelaced Story

GraceLaced blog was born in the summer of 2007 out of Ruth's simple desire to find God's grace laced through everyday life—to purposefully consider how her faith could intersect with all the seemingly mundane in life. At the time, she was a wife of nine years, a mother to three young boys, a church-planting pastor's wife, and a stay-at-home mom who had died to a few dreams along the way. With a degree in fine arts, a love of writing, and graduate work at seminary, life had turned out differently than she had anticipated. And so she wrote in the evenings, captured photos of all that was growing in and outside of her home life, and sought to find the thread that linked each seemingly mundane moment with the character of God and His work in her life…the thread of the gospel woven in the fabric of life's story.

In the fall of 2013, with baby boy number six on her lap, Ruth joined a 31-day blogging challenge hosted by The Nesting Place. The theme she chose for the month was "Drawing Close," which combined two of her passions: drawing/painting and nearness to God. She had recently joined Instagram and faithfully posted each day's #drawingclose offering with a small insight about walking with the Lord in connection with her artwork. By the month's end, she had received requests to purchase her art. She found new energy for drawing and painting, even with little ones in tow, because the artwork was now born out of a desire to reflect the Creator and not to fulfill her own dreams.

GraceLaced Shoppe opened its online doors in November 2013. To Ruth's surprise, her work and words began to spread and gain audience worldwide. Today, she's still the sole painter and the accompanying truth-teller behind the art in GraceLaced Shoppe and GraceLaced blog, championed by a small but mighty staff including her husband, Troy, who serves as Chief Operations Officer to the brand (but Chief Encouragement Officer to Ruth). Her team makes it possible for her to stay at the creative helm of the company while embracing how #motherhoodissanctifying with her six young sons at home. There, she continues to find grace laced through the everyday.

Ruth, through the ever-growing community of GraceLaced, shares beauty and truth with thousands daily, ships her art around the world regularly, and seeks to walk in truth, especially in the unseen places of her life…that she might reflect the One worthy of exalting in words and dazzling color.

Find Ruth—her art and heart—at gracelaced.com, and at @gracelaced on Instagram, Facebook, and Twitter.

acknowledgments

This book exists with grateful thanks to:

Troy...for gently instructing, by example, how to walk through every season of life with dependency and declaration of God's faithfulness. You shepherd me like no other.

Caleb, Liam, Judah, Stone, Asa, and Haddon...you are the wind in my sails.

The Chou and Simons families...for standing by our side, always. Mama and Baba, thanks for nurturing my gifts and believing in them.

Ruth...for walking this journey with me with care and perseverance.

Janelle and Betty...for patiently bringing my heart and my hands to life. And to my Harvest House family...thank you for trusting and investing in me.

My dedicated GraceLaced staff, present (Gina, Jessica, Caity, Sarah, Jordan, Hannah, Caleb) and past...for being the hands and feet that carry my heart beyond where I could ever go alone.

Tara and Taylor for supporting me so sacrificially—I could not have survived this season without you; Sayra and Sherry for continual encouragement; Becky for those faithful morning texts; Jamie for making every conversation count; Annie for lending your hands and heart in seen and unseen ways; Greg and Nancy for offering much more than production; Pat and Barbara for generously sharing your expertise and cheering me on; Karen, who marked the beginning with Spurgeon; and David, who held these pages first.

Ashley for helping me keep my eye on what's truly worthy; Joy for seeing and capturing the light, the unbreakable, and the truth of our tender season; Kara for championing my voice; to Christie for the poignant encouragement at the starting line; and Myquillin, who three years ago kinda caused it all to begin.

To those who started reading GraceLaced, the blog, ten years ago. Thank you for, together, finding the grace of God in the everyday. What a decade it's been.

And to a faithful and merciful God who causes us to tell His story uniquely, in spite of our weaknesses...thanks be to Him who is making all things new.

From him and through him and to him are all things. To him be glory forever. Amen.

ROMANS 11:36